**Published by Young Money
(part of Young Enterprise)**

Young Enterprise Head Office
Yeoman House
Sekforde St
London
EC1R 0HF

Young Enterprise is a registered charity.
Registered number 313697

© 2018 Young Money

ISBN 978-1-9164672-2-4

Printed in the United Kingdom by Geoff Neal Group.

British Library Cataloguing in Publication Data
A Catalogue record for this publication is available
from the British Library.

Acknowledgments

Young Money would li[...]
founder of MoneySavi[...]
donation, direction and passion that made this
project possible.

Young Money would also like to thank the teachers
and consultants who guided the development of
Your Money Matters, FedEx for kindly distributing the
textbook and this teacher's guide to schools in England
and the Department of Education for their help and
guidance in the development of this textbook.

In addition, special thanks to:

Contributing authors

Stewart Jones

Emma Waller

Russell Winnard, Young Money

Liz Booth, Young Money

Other contributors

Robyn Vernon-Harcourt, Young Money

Eileen Gannon, Young Money

Feyi Onamusi, Young Money

Charlotte Churchill, Young Money

Braden Clamp, Young Money

Design by **Something Big Ltd.**

Printed by **Geoff Neal Group**

Proofread by **Melissa Stewart**

ENSURE YOU'RE IN THE KNOWS,
NOT IN THE KNOW NOTS.

We live in one of the world's most competitive consumer economies. Companies spend billions on advertising, marketing and teaching their staff to sell – while consumers get no buyers training. This creates an imbalance that is devastating to the wellbeing of millions of people; and see scams, misselling, poor decisions and over-indebtedness in abundance.

I passionately believe financial education can redress that misbalance. That's why I campaigned long and hard to get it onto the national curriculum, which we achieved in 2014 (split across maths and citizenship).

Sadly though, that was a pyrrhic victory. A tick box exercise, which hasn't seen much change because schools have been thoroughly under-resourced. Teachers, both new and on-going, have had little training, and all this has put pressure on you and your school to deliver 'yet another' demand on you and your school's resources and time.

This isn't good enough for our children or our schools. So, having decided enough is enough, I've put my money where my mouth is and have funded the financial education charity Young Money (formerly pfeg) to create the very first financial education textbook for secondary schools.

Your Money Matters is mapped to the national curriculum and this teacher's guide will support your team to identify where financial education can be integrated into other areas of learning, so it doesn't unnecessarily require additional curriculum time, and can supporting existing delivery.

I hope this textbook and teacher's guide will empower you to provide quality, cutting-edge education on the issues students will face now and in the future.

Martin Lewis OBE
Founder of MoneySavingExpert.com

Young Money is very grateful to Martin Lewis OBE for funding the development and delivery of Your Money Matters and this teacher's guide into every English state secondary school.

YOUR MONEY
MATTERS

It's an increasingly complex world out there for young people, with a huge range of financial decisions that need to be taken from an early age, in the face of ever-increasing technological changes in the financial landscape. Your Money Matters aims to help young people get to grips with these money choices, which have such an important impact on the future of your young people. We couldn't have produced Your Money Matters and this teacher's guide without Martin Lewis OBE, who funded its development and delivery, and we're extremely grateful for his support. I'd also like to thank the many dedicated teachers who contributed to the APPG Report 'Financial Education in Schools: Two Years On – Job Done' highlighting the need for this textbook, which provides teachers with a high-quality teaching resource to support and enhance financial education delivery. I very much hope that Your Money Matters goes a long way to helping your young people prepare for their financial futures.

Michal Mercieca,
CEO of Young Money, which is part of the charity Young Enterprise

Contact
Young Enterprise Head Office
Yeoman House
Sekforde St
London
EC1R 0HF

T. 020 7330 9470
E. info@y-m.org.uk

Follow us on twitter @YoungMoneyEdu

YOUR MONEY MATTERS
A TEACHER'S GUIDE

This Teacher's Guide accompanies the **Your Money Matters** textbook produced by Young Money.

Your Money Matters is a student-facing textbook for Key Stage 4 students. It is mapped to the national curriculum, has been trialled with teachers and students, and is a Quality Mark resource.

It has been developed to support schools to deliver a coherent programme of financial education, providing all students with the essential knowledge, skills and attitudes towards money as they transition into greater independence.

What is financial education?

Financial education is the teaching and learning that leads to individuals improving their **knowledge, skills** and **attitudes** in relation to money and money matters. Through receiving high quality financial education an individual would be expected to develop and improve their **financial capability**.

The teaching of financial education occurs in a variety of ways within schools, such as stand-alone qualifications, embedded within certain subject areas and as part of discrete off-timetable activities. However individual schools choose to deliver financial education, it should form part of a planned programme of study, which builds on prior knowledge and reinforces learning throughout secondary school.

Why financial education is needed

Children and young people growing up today are exposed to an increasing range of financial decisions, from day-to-day activities, such as whether or not to download apps and music online, through to longer-term decisions, such as how to finance a car purchase, and whether to attend university or look for employment.

The financial and consumer landscape in which young people grow up has changed dramatically in recent years. Technological change has facilitated their involvement in making financial decisions from an early age and fundamentally changed their concept of money as compared with previous generations.

Financial education can play an important role in helping young people navigate these new financial and consumer landscapes and helps prepare them for the financial reality of life beyond the school gates.

Financial education in the school curriculum

Financial education has been a statutory part of the English secondary school national curriculum since 2014. It is statutory within citizenship and as a context for learning within mathematics. In addition, many schools deliver financial education through PSHE education (personal, social, health and economic education). Although the "economic" element of PSHE is non-statutory, it is something which many schools choose to deliver. The PSHE Association has developed a Programme of Study for PSHE Education at Key Stage 4 that makes explicit references to many aspects of financial education.

Where is financial education on the national curriculum?

1. Mathematics (statutory)

The purpose of study in the mathematics programme of study clearly states that it is necessary to prepare students to be **financially literate**.

The national curriculum for mathematics aims, state that students should apply their mathematical knowledge in **financial contexts**.

This aim is explicitly referenced in the section on solving problems – **"students should develop their use of formal mathematical knowledge to interpret and solve problems, including in financial contexts"**.

2. Citizenship (statutory)

The purpose of study in the citizenship programme of study (key stages 3 and 4) states that it should **prepare students to manage their money well**.

The stated aims of the citizenship programme of study state that the curriculum should enable all students to **manage their money on a day-to-day basis and plan for future financial needs**.

Under the Key Stage 4 subject content the following core statement explicitly refers to **money and finance**:

"Students should be taught about:

Income and expenditure, credit and debt, insurance, savings and pensions, financial products and services, and how public money is raised and spent".

3. Personal, social, health and economic education (non-statutory)

In the PSHE education programme of study, core theme 3: "Living in the Wider World", and the associated learning opportunities, contain explicit references to **financial education**.

At key stages 3 and 4 this core theme focuses on:

- **Rights and responsibilities as members of diverse communities, as active citizens and participants in the local and national economy**
- **How to make informed choices and be enterprising and ambitious**
- **How to develop employability, team working and leadership skills and develop flexibility and resilience**
- **The economic and business environment**
- **How personal financial choices can affect oneself and others and about rights and responsibilities as consumers.**

Suggested Key Stage 4 learning opportunities include:

"Students should have the opportunity to learn:

- **About changing patterns of employment (local, national, European and global)**
- **About different types of business, how they are organised and financed**
- **To recognise and manage the influences on their financial decisions (including managing risk, planning for expenditure, understanding debt and gambling in all its forms)**
- **To access appropriate support for financial decision-making and for concerns over money, gambling etc.**
- **To be a critical consumer of goods and services (including financial services) and recognise the wider impact of their purchasing choices**
- **Their consumer rights and how to seek redress"**.

In practice, many schools deliver financial education in a cross-curricular manner, teaching it in mathematics, citizenship and PSHE education and then supplementing their work during the school year with off-timetable activities. This textbook has been designed to be used in all of these contexts.

The Financial Education Planning Framework

Young Money has developed two frameworks that aim to support the planning, teaching and progression of financial education by setting out the key areas of financial knowledge, skills and attitudes, across four core themes:

- How to manage money
- Becoming a critical consumer
- Managing risks and emotions associated with money
- Understanding the important role money plays in our lives.

The first framework is aimed at ages 3-11 (key stages 1 and 2) and the second framework is aimed at ages 11-19 (key stages 3, 4 and 5).

Secondary teachers who are developing a financial education programme of study can use the Secondary Planning Framework to identify the financial education knowledge, skills and attitudes appropriate for their students and then use the textbook to support the delivery of outcomes from the planning framework.

Teachers will find that the textbook and Secondary Planning Framework regularly complement each other. For example, teachers wishing to teach 'managing risks and emotions associated with money – dealing with fraud' (from the planning framework 14-16 years) will find the chapter on security and fraud provides information and activities that will enable delivery of all related outcomes.

How to use Your Money Matters

Your Money Matters aims to build the skills, knowledge and attitudes of young people to make informed choices about managing their money, now and in the future.

There are six chapters on topics relevant to Key Stage 4 students. Each chapter will start with a question, which the information included in the chapter will help the students answer.

In addition, in each chapter you will find:

INFORMATION
The information icon highlights key and useful information on the chapter topic.

DID YOU KNOW?
We have included interesting and thought-provoking facts related to the topics covered.

ACTIVITY
The activities are intended for students to complete to help build their knowledge and understanding of money matters.

DISCUSSION
The discussions provide an opportunity for students to discuss the topic areas and give their opinions and thoughts to help develop and consider their attitudes towards money and money matters.

CASE STUDY
The case studies provide real and relevant examples, which can be used to explore the topics in more detail, providing an opportunity for students to work through the scenario and decide the best course of action.

QUESTIONS
Comprehension questions are provided at the end of each section giving students the opportunity to check their understanding.

WHAT HAVE YOU LEARNT?
Each chapter is summarised with a 'What have you learnt?' section, which includes summary activities and case studies for students to complete, drawing on the knowledge they have gained throughout the chapter.

FURTHER YOUR KNOWLEDGE
At the end of each chapter, there is an additional section which includes further and more detailed information about the subject area, and extension activities to stretch more-able students.

Aims of the Teacher's Guide

Whatever the delivery method of financial education within a school there are ideas, exercises and challenges within Your Money Matters that will enable teachers to supplement existing practice, or to develop a planned programme of financial education that will help young people navigate the ever-changing financial and consumer landscapes they face.

The aims of this Teacher's Guide are:

- To provide guidance on how to use Your Money Matters to plan and deliver financial education

- To support the teaching and embedding of financial education within the curriculum by highlighting learning opportunities and potential cross-curricular and extra-curricular activities

- To signpost to further support on the topics covered in the textbook.

The Teacher's Guide has six chapters, which reflect the six financial education topics covered by Your Money Matters:

1. SAVING

2. MAKING THE MOST OF YOUR MONEY

3. BORROWING

4. MOVING ON FROM SCHOOL – THE WORLD OF WORK

5. RISK AND REWARD

6. SECURITY AND FRAUD

Within each chapter there is an outline of the topic and why it is important, plus a detailed curriculum map identifying where these topics can be delivered within different subjects.

Your Money Matters has been developed to be used with year 10 students, but many schools may well decide to use the textbook with other year groups, because schools tend to be at different stages when delivering financial education to their students.

Using the Lesson Plan Builder

For each of the Your Money Matters chapters the Teacher's Guide provides a **Lesson Plan Builder**. This consists of a set of starter, core and extension activities that all build on information and activities with the textbook. These have been designed to enable teachers to build a 45-60 minute lesson that uses elements from the chapter to support learning:

1. Select a starter activity to introduce the lesson

2. Choose a core activity to develop learning

3. If time allows, pick an extension activity to progress learning

The activities within the starter, core and extension steps can be matched together in a wide range of combinations in order to develop lessons appropriate for the needs of different groups of students, both in terms of ability and activity.

Please note, the financial information in this book was accurate at the time of writing (August 2018) but may change, for instance when the government updates yearly allowance figures, or if new legislation is introduced.

Question answers

At the end of each chapter of the Teacher's Guide, you can find the answers to the activities included within the textbook chapter, including the 'Further your knowledge' questions. You can also find guidance and areas to consider when addressing the case studies and discussions with your students for that chapter.

YOUR MONEY MATTERS
A TEACHERS GUIDE
CONTENTS

SAVING

What does this chapter cover?

This chapter considers the reasons why people save money, how to compare the savings options available and why saving is an important way of reaching future financial goals.

The following topics are explored either through the provision of information and case studies, or through activities for students. Alongside each topic is a possible curriculum link:

TOPIC	CURRICULUM LINK					
	PSHE				CITIZENSHIP	MATHEMATICS
	MANAGING RISK	PLANNING FOR EXPENDITURE	UNDERSTANDING DEBT	BEING A CRITICAL CONSUMER		
What saving means	■	■	■		■	
Reasons for saving	■	■	■		■	
Ways of saving	■	■	■	■	■	
Interest rates and AER	■	■		■	■	■
Types of savings account	■	■		■	■	■
Money and mental health	■	■		■		

WHY IS THIS TOPIC IMPORTANT FOR YOUNG PEOPLE?

55% of young people aged 20-29 **worry about being able to save.**

Source: www.nationwide.co.uk

Almost **10 MILLION** households in the UK have **no savings whatsoever.**

Source: The Money Charity 2017

81% of 18-24 year olds do not understand the term **"interest rate".**

Source: MoneySuperMarket research 2017

LESSON PLAN BUILDER

There are references to borrowing in some of these suggested activities as the topics are closely linked. You may wish to refer to the Borrowing chapter of Your Money Matters and the Teacher's Guide for additional support on this chapter.

Step 1 – Pick a starter activity

(10 – 15 minutes)

Reasons for saving PSHE CITIZENSHIP

Ask students to write a list of items they feel they need to save for a) this year b) over the next 10 years. This can be used to start a discussion on the reasons why people save (see page 12) and then be combined with the core activity on **Saving situations in Step 2.**

There may also be the possibility to follow up with a brief discussion on issues such as:

- Are they concerned about saving in the next 10 years?
- Are they expecting to fund their own car, higher education, first home?
- Where do they keep their savings?
- Where has the money come from?

Alternatively, give the students the reasons why people save and then use the discussion question on reasons to save (see page 12) as a starter.

Delayed gratification PSHE CITIZENSHIP MATHEMATICS

To introduce the concept of delayed gratification, ask the students to consider the following dilemma. You have won first prize at your school spelling bee competition. You have two choices for the prize:

- **Option 1:** Take £20 home today
- **Option 2:** Take home £1.83 a day for the next 15 days

In pairs, ask the students to calculate which option earns more money and by how much more. Then ask them to consider which option they would choose and why. Follow this with a whole class discussion about the benefits of delayed gratification and introduce the information on page 12.

Why some people do not save PSHE CITIZENSHIP

Instead of thinking about why people save (see page 12) you could ask students why many people do **not** save. Collect their reasons and ask them to list their three top tips for someone who is finding it difficult to save. Take feedback and try to agree on the top three tips. Produce a poster to display this at the front of the class or ask students to produce it – possibly as homework.

Terms and definitions `PSHE` `CITIZENSHIP`

As students complete the work in the Saving chapter you could test their understanding at the start of a new lesson by asking them to create their own starter activity. They should write out five key savings terms on one set of cards and then create a separate set of cards with the definitions on. They can then swap with another team to peer assess each other's understanding of key terms and definitions. Get the students to match the terms with the definitions. 10 examples of terms from the chapter are: saving, savings, delayed gratification, credit union, current account, interest, AER, ISA, notice.

Show their answers to the class and ask if they feel they are correct. This could be a good starter to do at any time, for example, before the core activities on **creating and choosing a savings account in Step 2.**

A game of taboo `PSHE` `CITIZENSHIP`

Split the group into teams and give each team 2 minutes to pick a key saving term and discuss how to explain it without actually saying the term. Nominate one member of each team to describe the term to the rest of the class and see if they can guess it.

Step 2 – Pick a core activity/activities
(25 – 30 minutes)

Saving situations `PSHE` `CITIZENSHIP` `MATHEMATICS`

The activity on Sam and Jakob (see page 13) could form one of a range of possible scenarios that students could work on in pairs or groups before feeding back their answers to the whole class. Other scenarios could be devised around saving or spending situations, for example:

- An 18-year-old wants a new games console – should they save, borrow from family or buy on credit from a games shop?

- A 15-year-old has a part-time job paying £30 per week. They want some new trainers costing £60 but owe money to their mum and to a friend – should they save up, pay off their debts or borrow more from mum and pay off what they owe later?

Similar short scenarios could be created so that students can look at three different ones.

You may wish to refer to the Borrowing chapter of Your Money Matters and the Teacher's Guide for additional support on this activity.

Calculating interest `PSHE` `CITIZENSHIP` **MATHEMATICS**

Use the worked example (see page 15) to demonstrate to students how interest is calculated. Depending on ability, you could then ask students to either complete the questions that use the simple interest formula (see page 15) or the questions that use the compound interest formula (see page 17).

Create a savings account `PSHE` `CITIZENSHIP`

Use the table on savings accounts features (see page 20) to explain the terminology associated with them – like notice period, easy access, savings bonds and ISA.

Then get the students to work in pairs or small groups to create a new savings account that they think would appeal to young people. They could use the features in the table and add extras that they think would attract people to the account e.g. maybe some free gifts?

They should give their account a name and then feed back to the class. You could collate the key features of each account onto a table at the front of the class and then ask the students to vote for which one appeals to them the most. They cannot vote for their own!

Choosing a savings account `PSHE` `CITIZENSHIP`

Use the activity (see page 22) on three young people looking to set up a savings account. Students should complete the four questions at the start of the activity and record their answers in a table. You could go through the first young person with them and stress the importance of giving reasons for their choices. Then ask the students to complete their answers for the other two young people.

As they complete their table, ask them to use their imagination to create another individual who would be suited to an account that they have not already chosen as an appropriate one.

Alternatively, they could write a paragraph to describe themselves, as in the activity, and then decide which of the accounts is the most appropriate one for them.

Money and mental health `PSHE`

Use the activity about Abby and Paul (page 28) to introduce how someone's financial situation can affect their mental health. Ask students to come up with a list of other financial situations that might lead to a mental health problem (e.g. going into debt due to losing your job) and then to suggest how these problems can be overcome.

This could also be followed up with a whole class discussion about the physical and emotional symptoms of mental health issues caused by a financial problem. Finally, ask students (or conduct research) to consider where individuals could go to seek financial help and support if a friend or family member is struggling with financial worries.

Step 3 – Pick an extension activity
(10 – 15 minutes)

Savings account research

If students have access to the internet they can research and evaluate the features of three different young people's savings accounts (e.g. one from a bank, one from a building society).

They might compare: the interest rate on each account; the minimum required to open the account; any restrictions on making withdrawals from the account; and special introductory offers on each account.

Savings research

Students could devise a questionnaire to carry out some research on savings habits of their friends and classmates. This could be done individually or in pairs and could include questions like:

* Do you have a savings account?
* How often do you save?
* Why do you save?

Students should be advised not to ask direct personal questions like, "how much you have saved?".

Saving in other ways

Ask students to think about other ways of saving money that they could do as a class.

This could include making sure that the lights are switched off when they leave the room to save electricity, collecting and recycling cans and bottles, or saving paper by doing tasks digitally if possible.

Task them to try and do as many of these as possible over the course of a week or a month.

Step 4 – Links for further information and extra-curricular opportunities

Extra-curricular opportunities

In addition to the activities identified above there are many opportunities for young people to do work on this topic outside of the curriculum.

Examples include:

* Visiting local financial institutions and collecting information on their savings accounts for young people.

* Using a comparison website to compare different savings accounts based on a set amount of savings (e.g. £100) to see how much interest they would earn. Students can also explore how the accounts differ aside from the interest.

Links

* www.moneysavingexpert.com
* www.fca.org.uk
* www.moneyandmentalhealth.org

ANSWERS:

DISCUSSION: REASONS FOR SAVING **PAGE 12**

- For a very specific purpose or to help achieve a particular goal – e.g. wedding, holiday

- To gather together wealth for future use – e.g. for retirement, to purchase property

- To put money aside for unplanned events – e.g. car breaks down and needs fixing, kitchen appliance needs replacing

- To keep your money safe – money lying around can easily be taken, too tempting and easily spent if not kept in a safe place.

ACTIVITY: DELAYED GRATIFICATION **PAGE 13**

Question 1:

a) 16 weeks

b) Weekly cost of 52 weeks = £260 - £80 for annual payment = £180 saving.

c) Yes – Sam gets to save £180 and will have the satisfaction of having saved for it.

d) He has to wait 16 weeks to get it and won't be able to stream anything for 16 weeks whilst he is saving. It may increase in price during the 16 weeks.

Question 2:

a)

	OPTION 1 – BUY NOW FOR £45	OPTION 2 – BUY IN 3 MONTHS FOR £55 WITH EXTRAS
Benefit	• Cheaper – save £10 • Get to play the game now	• Receive all bonus levels and games • Once available, easy to download (don't have to wait for the disc to be delivered)
Implications	• Don't get the added features and levels	• Need to save an extra £10 • Have to wait 3 months to play the game • More expensive

b) Based on the answers to question a) students will be able to determine what, in their opinion, Jakob should do.

ACTIVITY: SIMPLE INTEREST **PAGE 15**

Question 1:

a) £1,000 x 0.02 x 3 = £60

b) £1,000 x 0.02 x 7 = £140

c) £1,000 x 0.02 x 15 = £300

Question 2:

Interest is not accruing if more money is saved into the account. It is only being added to the principal amount not the amount saved at the end of each year.

ACTIVITY: COMPOUND INTEREST **PAGE 17**

COMPOUND INTEREST METHOD	SIMPLE INTEREST METHOD
1a) £150,000 x 1.035 = £173,891 £173, 891 - £150,000 = £23,891	**3a)** £150,000 x 0.03 x 5 = £22,500
1b) £150,000 x 1.0312 = £213,864 £213,864 - £150,000 = £63,864	**3b)** £150,000 x 0.03 x 12 = £54,000
1c) £150,000 x 1.0320 = £270,917 £270,917 - £150,000 = £120,917	**3c)** £150,000 x 0.03 x 20 = £90,000
2a) £150,000 x 1.055 = £191,442 £191,442 - £150,000 = £41,442	£150,000 x 0.05 x 5 = £37,500
2b) £150,000 x 1.0512 = £269,378 £269,378 - £150,000 = £119,378	£150,000 x 0.05 x 12 = £90,000
2c) £150,000 x 1.0520 = £397,995 £397,995 - £150,000 = £247,995	£150,000 x 0.05 x 20 = £150,000

As you would expect, the compound interest method yields more interest as it is accruing annually rather than at the end of the savings period. Therefore, the compound interest method is more beneficial for the saver.

 ACTIVITY: UK INTEREST RATES **PAGE 17**

1. There has been a gradual decline in interest on savings from 1990 to 2017. In 1990 the average savings interest rate in the UK was approximately 13.8% and by 2017 it had declined to approximately 1%.

2. £1,000 x 0.138 x 1 = £138 interest

3. £1,000 x 0.01 x 1 = £10 interest

4. The reduction in savings interest rates has meant that savers now receive considerably less interest on their savings. This makes putting money into a savings account less attractive in terms of the interest it will accrue.

5. Since 2009, savings interest rates have hovered around 1%-2%, with rates on some accounts often far lower. These rates are likely to remain low until a significant change in the UK economy.

 DISCUSSION: INTEREST RATES **PAGE 18**

• Bank balances fluctuate daily because deposits and withdrawals are made on a regular basis, therefore it makes sense to pay interest on the amount of money that is in the account on a daily basis. However, you may only be credited once a month because the cost in administration of paying everyone daily would be too high.

• To maximise profit and to remain competitive with other institutions.

ACTIVITY: WHY DO BANKS PAY INTEREST? **PAGE 18**

1. 9.5% - 1.5% = 8% x £2,000 = £160

Or another way of calculating it is the saver gets £30 interest (£2,000 x 0.015 x 1) and the borrower pays £190 (£2,000 x 0.95 x 1), so the bank gets £190 from the borrower and pays the saver £30 so the bank have made £160 profit.

2. The bank would make a loss i.e. the bank would be paying more to savers than the revenue collected from the borrowers.

 ## ACTIVITY: CHOOSING WHAT'S RIGHT FOR YOU **PAGE 22**

Junior Plush Account – Gene because he is 15 and doesn't meet the requirements of the other accounts.

Plush One Account – Nandita because she only needs the money in 6 months' time so can give 30 days' notice, she is over 16 and earns a minimum of £75 per month to open the account.

Super Plush Account – Adi because it has the highest interest rate, he has £100 to open the account and he earns £50 per month.

 ## ACTIVITY: HOW TO GET THE MONEY TO SAVE **PAGE 25**

1. Going to university, buying a house, wedding, birth of a child, going on holiday, buying a car.

2. Costs will depend on students' expectations and prior knowledge but should be realistic.

3. Opening a savings account or an ISA, putting together a savings plan – how can you cut spending, increase earnings and get best value deals.

4. Unexpected bills arrive, additional events arise that could not be predicted, price of items increase, personal priorities change over time, external factors change (e.g. rise or fall in interest rates affecting savings).

5. Spread risk across different savings methods, start planning/saving now.

6. Students may find their estimates in costs are higher/ lower than predicted, may possibly feel that saving is not a priority at the moment and may think that the amount they want to save is unattainable in the short or medium term.

CASE STUDY: SAVING SCENARIOS PAGE 26

Wasim

- Sell the trainers that he does not wear any more (e.g. online auction/selling sites)
- Arrange to do some paid work around the house for his mum, dad or other family members
- Set aside any monetary gifts that he may receive to fund his new purchase
- Consider getting a part-time job at the weekends to pay for his expensive tastes
- Open a savings account to keep his money safe or put the cash in a money jar so he can see his money accumulate
- If Wasim chooses not to save, he won't be able to buy the trainers.

Chloe

- Set a budget and save a proportion of her income every week
- Open an easy access savings account so that the money is stored safely, and she can access it quickly if needed
- Save any monetary gifts she receives throughout the year
- If she chooses not to save, she may have insufficient funds for any emergencies that occur. This may lead to her having to borrow which may come at a cost.

Ayomide

- Use his savings to pay for the holiday because the cost of borrowing on a credit card is greater than the interest received on the savings
- HOWEVER, if he chooses not to save up for the holiday or use his existing savings and uses his credit card to pay for the holiday instead this gives him greater consumer protection if the holiday firm goes bankrupt, so he is more likely to get his money back. Once his bill comes through, he could then use his savings to pay the holiday off so that he doesn't incur any charges/interest. He should not use his credit card to exchange for currency as this may incur much higher rates of interest (depending on the credit card)
- Apply for a pre-paid currency card which allows him to load the card with money before he goes on holiday so that he is not carrying large quantities of cash around. This way he can only spend what is on the card. He can use this just like a debit card to pay for goods while away from home
- As he seems to be sensible about saving, Ayomide could always start saving again once he is back home and build up his savings again.

ACTIVITY: SAVING PLAN **PAGE 27**

1.

- I am saving for driving lessons
- I need £140
- It will take me 5 months.

DATE	I PLAN TO SAVE (£)	HOW WILL I SAVE THIS?	I STILL NEED TO SAVE (£)
January	£10	Pocket money I get from Nan	£130
February	£30	Birthday money	£100
February	£10	Pocket money I get from Nan	£90
March	£20	Chores around the house – washing car, cleaning room and taking dog for a walk	£70
March	£10	Pocket money from Nan	£60
April	£15	Bus fare savings	£45
April	£10	Pocket money from Nan	£35
May	£10	Sale of trainers	£25
May	£15	Bus fare savings	£10
May	£10	Pocket money from Nan	£0

2.

- May

3.

- Nan is unable to give him his pocket money
- He decides not to help around the house
- He doesn't receive the birthday money that he expects
- He still gets the bus
- He doesn't sell his trainers
- He decides to spend what he saves on other things.

4.

- Get a part time job and save a proportion every week or month
- Set up a savings account or a cash ISA that he can top up regularly
- Ensure that he gets the best value for money by researching prices
- Sell any other unwanted items that he might have.

 CASE STUDY: MONEY AND MENTAL HEALTH **PAGE 28**

1.
- Anxiety and low mood
- Worry and inability to sleep, leading to tiredness
- Depression
- Headaches
- Panic attacks
- Feeling of shame and embarrassment
- May lead to ill health (e.g. high blood pressure, poor diet).

2.
- Feeling of not being able to get on top of the bills, therefore feeling unable to plan for the future
- Effect on relationship e.g. arguments
- Effect on work e.g. poor concentration
- Unable to make good decisions
- May be more likely to bury head in the sand and not deal with the problem.

3.
- Save little and often and aim for about £300 just in case the washing machine needs replacing
- Put it somewhere where they can't dip into it (e.g. bank or savings account)
- Ask for help if you need to (e.g. Citizens Advice or Money Advice Service)
- Tell the bank and people they owe money to about the situation
- Cancel the holiday, if possible, and go on it when they have saved for it.

ANSWERS:
FURTHER YOUR KNOWLEDGE

COMPOUND INTEREST PAGE 30

	PRINCIPAL DEPOSITED	INTEREST RATE	COMPOUND PERIOD	NUMBER OF YEARS	INTEREST
a	£3,000	2.5%	Quarterly	6	£483.87
b	£6,500	3.25%	Weekly	4	£909.81
c	£8,325	2.76%	Daily	7	£1,784.13

Work out how much interest will have accrued in the following savings accounts:

a) Write in the figures:
   Calculate the bracketed figures:

   Multiply the final two figures:

$£3,000 (1 + 0.025/4)4 (6)$
$£3,000 (1.00625)24$
$£3,000 (1.16129)$
£3,483.87 (£3,000 principal and £483.87 interest)

b) Write in the figures:
   Calculate the bracketed figures:

   Multiply the final two figures:

$£6,500 (1 + 0.0325/52)52 (4)$
$£6,500 (1.00063)208$
$£6,500 (1.13997)$
£7,409.81 (£6,500 principal and £909.81 interest)

c) Write in the figures:
   Calculate the bracketed figures:

   Multiply the final two figures:

$£8,325 (1 + 0.0276/365)365 (7)$
$£8,325 (1.000076)2,555$
$£8,325 (1.21431)$
£10,109.13 (£8,325 principal and £1,784.13 interest)
(Figures have been rounded)

PERSONAL SAVINGS ALLOWANCE PAGE 31

1. Zane will save £600 in the course of a year (£50 x 12 months). Total savings at the end of the year will be £2,600 (£2,000 + £600). The interest on these savings will be £40.30 (1.55% of £2,600). This is a long way short of the £1,000 PSA allowed to basic rate tax payers so he will not have to pay any tax on the interest earned by his savings.

2. The interest on Camila's savings will be £1,320 (2.2% of £60,000). This is £320 more than the £1,000 PSA allowed to basic rate tax payers, so she will pay tax on the latter amounting to £64 (20% of £320).

3. The interest on Ali's savings will be:
- Account A: £525
- Account B: £100
- Account C: £4

Total interest on Ali's savings comes to £629. This is £129 above the £500 PSA allowed to higher rate tax payers. His tax bill on his savings will come to £51.60 (40% of £129).

4. Ava and Will's joint savings account interest will be £646 and this is considered to be split equally between them (£323 each). Ava's separate account will earn £325 interest making a total of £648. As a higher rate tax payer this is £148 over the £500 limit so £59.20 (40% of £148) will need to be paid. Will's separate account will generate £272 making a total of £595 but as a basic rate tax payer this is below the £1,000 threshold so there is nothing to pay. The ISAs interest is irrelevant as this is separate to the PSA.

MAKING THE MOST OF YOUR MONEY

What does this chapter cover?

This chapter considers what factors influence the choices that young people might make when spending money and how to manage the choices that are made.

The following topics are explored either through the provision of information and case studies, or through activities for students. Alongside each topic is a possible curriculum link:

TOPIC	CURRICULUM LINK					
	PSHE				CITIZENSHIP	MATHEMATICS
	PLANNING FOR EXPENDITURE	UNDERSTANDING DEBT	BE A CRITICAL CONSUMER	CONSUMER RIGHTS AND REDRESS		
Needs and wants	✓		✓		✓	
Influences on spending	✓		✓		✓	
Ways to pay	✓	✓			✓	
Budgeting	✓				✓	✓
Value for money	✓		✓		✓	✓
Unit prices	✓	✓	✓		✓	✓
Consumer rights	✓	✓	✓	✓	✓	

WHY IS THIS TOPIC IMPORTANT FOR YOUNG PEOPLE?

Only **39%** of young people aged 14-17 often or always plan how they are going to buy the things they need.

Source: The Financial Capability of Children, Young People and their Parents in the UK, The Money Advice Service March 2017

77% of people aged 25-34 made contactless payments during **2017**.

Source: UK Payments Market Summary, June 2018

LESSON PLAN BUILDER

There are references to borrowing in some of these suggested activities as the topics are closely linked. You may wish to refer to the Borrowing chapter of Your Money Matters and the Teacher's Guide for additional support on this chapter.

Step 1 – Pick a starter activity
(10 – 15 minutes)

Needs and wants PSHE CITIZENSHIP

Ask students what they would buy if they had £100 per month available to them. Take answers and collate at the front of the class. How many items on the list are essential? What is meant by a need and a want? Can they give an example of each?

Influences on spending PSHE CITIZENSHIP

Display the list of influences (see page 35) at the front of the class. Ask students who or what will have the biggest influence on them when they decide to buy particular products. Read out 5-10 products one at a time (e.g. a new pair of trainers, a new smartphone, tickets to see a live band) and take a poll of the biggest influence on spending for each product. Discuss why the influence might change depending on the product. Students may also want to suggest other influences not on the list.

How to pay PSHE CITIZENSHIP

Link this to the work on ways to pay (see page 38). Ask students to think of two pros and two cons of each method of payment. Ask students to identify situations or scenarios where each method of payment would be most suitable and ask them to give reasons for their answers. For example, the most suitable method for paying for concert tickets may be using PayPal as it is secure and safe.

Branding PSHE CITIZENSHIP

A search of logo images online should yield enough pictures to make a short quiz for students to "guess the well-known logo". Some quiz sites will have sets of questions already done. When the quiz is complete, discuss the power of brands with students and link to the work you will be doing on value for money. Alternatively, ask students to name their favourite brands and what it is about them that they like. These can be any type of product: food, clothes, sports equipment, entertainment, etc. Then discuss why these brands are so powerful.

Unit price PSHE CITIZENSHIP MATHEMATICS

Use the short activity on the chicken and the egg (see page 47) as a starter to work on value for money. It is important to discuss whether unit price is the only factor that would help you decide on the best deal.

Step 2 – Pick a core activity/activities
(25 – 30 minutes)

Digital targeted marketing PSHE CITIZENSHIP

In groups, ask students to think of (or research) three ways that businesses use digital marketing to influence our buying habits (examples may include blogging/vlogging, social media advertising, email, website SEO, pop ups and use of apps). Once they have done this, they could then discuss how these methods influence their buying habits and rank them in order of most influential to least and explain why they feel this. Finally, each group could compare their answers to the rest of the class – which were the most/least influential methods for the class as a whole?

Budgeting PSHE CITIZENSHIP MATHEMATICS

After discussing the budgeting process and completing Robyn and Awurabena's budgets (see page 40 and 42) ask students to analyse the benefits and implications of personal budgeting. Follow this up with a whole class discussion about the advantages and potential pitfalls of personal budgeting.

In pairs, ask students to develop their own case study on budgeting. Their case studies must include an interesting scenario, information about the person's income and expenditure (so that a budget can be worked out) and at least three questions (including a maths style question) to answer. If there is time, ask students to type up their case study and include images to make it look appealing. Use the case studies to swap around the class for more budgeting practice.

Note: Students should be made aware that they shouldn't reveal information about their own personal circumstances when developing their case study.

Influences on spending PSHE CITIZENSHIP

Use the discussion about spending influences on different age groups (see page 35) and then complete the social media profiles activity (see page 36). Once the questions on page 37 have been answered, put students in pairs and get them to write the social media profile for a fictional character of their own creation. They will need to think about the character's activities and interests, favourite music, books, movies and television. Once they have completed the social media profile for their fictional character, ask them to answer the questions from the original profiles on page 36.

Consumer responsibility `PSHE` `CITIZENSHIP`

Following on from the work on influences on spending (see page 35), explain to students that as consumers they can follow some basic practices to try to ensure they get the best deal. Suggest an expensive product they are likely to buy now, or in the next few years, e.g. a new smartphone or tablet. Ask students to suggest five things they should do/find out before making the purchase. Examples include: using a comparison website to get the best price, reading reviews of the product, reading the small print about a product, finding out if the product is compatible with other products, finding out if the product has essential ongoing costs. They should rank these in importance and produce a set of guidelines. If possible, students should then put these guidelines into practice and carry out the research into a particular product.

Discuss with students whether consumer responsibility is something that people take seriously. Why is it that some people do not follow the guidelines that they have produced?

Value for money `PSHE` `CITIZENSHIP` `MATHEMATICS`

Ask students to complete the activity on brands (see page 45) and calculate the saving differences. Discuss with students what could be bought if there was a switch from the luxury brand to the value range. Then ask students what affects value for money when buying other products such as a car. In addition to price, they should also consider factors such as: quality of product, resale value, running costs, supplier experience, and availability of parts. Discuss with them whether the value for money for some goods will mainly be to do with price or other factors?.

Step 3 – Pick an extension activity
(10 – 15 minutes)

Where to go for help?

Students should find out which organisation(s) they would go to if they wanted to complain about a product.

Value for money deals

Ask students to create some examples of "good" and "bad" value for money deals. They could then test friends/family to spot the good deals and the bad deals. An example of a good deal could be a single can of cola costs 60p or buy a pack of eight for £4.00 and a bad deal would be a pizza costs £1.50 or buy two for £5.00 and get one free.

Price comparison sites

Visit a number of price comparison sites and find the best deals for the following products/services:

- 5-year loan of £10,000
- Brand new car
- Flight to Hong Kong
- Games console

Ask students to consider how easy it was to find the best deals, what are the problems with using price comparison sites, and what advice they would give to their friends about using price comparison sites.

Step 4 – Links for further information and extra-curricular opportunities

Extra-curricular opportunities

In addition to the activities identified in the lesson plan builder, there are many opportunities for young people to do work on this topic outside of the curriculum.

Examples include:

- Students use a comparison website to find the best price for the latest designer clothes or shoes they would like to buy.
- Students create a "top tips" list for planning a budget

- Ensure students are using their new-found budgeting and value for money skills around the school e.g. within the school council, planning school trips, preparing budgets for food technology and design technology.

Links

- www.citizensadvice.org.uk
- www.gov.uk/find-local-trading-standards-office
- https://www.moneysavingexpert.com/banking/Budget-planning/

ANSWERS:

DISCUSSION: NEEDS AND WANTS **PAGE 34**

Need argument – vital for keeping in contact with people, can't live without it, holds all my important information and details.

Want argument – do not have to use a smartphone to communicate with others, it is not a necessity, it is a luxury item.

Student views will change depending on the age of the individual, where they live and the amount of money they have.

DISCUSSION: INFLUENCES ON SPENDING **PAGE 35**

7-year-old – family, peers, seasonal

14-year-old – family, peers, advertising

25-year-old – disposable income, advertising, peers, culture

ACTIVITY: INFLUENCES ON SPENDING PAGE 36

1. **Jenaya** – social media, peers, family

   Simon – disposable income, advertising, seasonal

   Connie – disposable income, family, culture

2. **Simon –** most, **Jenaya** – least. More disposable income may mean that you are more likely to spend money on things you don't really need or may decide to save money, having less disposable income may mean you prioritise spending on things that you really need and go without the things you don't.

3. **Jenaya** – may affect where and how she spends her money, potentially spending money on things she doesn't really need or want.

4. Yes, it helps advertisers maximise their sales and profits by advertising to the people who are most likely to buy their products.

DISCUSSION: WAYS TO PAY PAGE 38

Discussions may be focused around:

Yes, it should be raised because it is more convenient, you get served in shops quicker and queuing takes less time. However, an increase in the limit benefits businesses more than the consumer.

No, it shouldn't be raised because people may end up spending more than they need to just because it's easier and quicker. It gives more incentive to criminals so fraudulent use may go up as they could get £50 of goods rather than £30 of goods for the same work.

DISCUSSION: DEVELOPMENTS IN MONEY **PAGE 39**

Discussions may be focused around:

Discussions around the next developments in money may focus around:

- Development of mobile wallets
- Codes instead of cards
- Wearable payment devices
- Home devices for payments (e.g. Amazon Echo, Google Home)
- AI (artificial intelligence) to detect fraudulent behaviour patterns and suspicious activities
- Development of biometric security

Discussion around whether it is or isn't possible to have a cashless society could include:

YES	NO
Fewer people now carry cash and make more payments by card.	Increase in fraud.
Save the economy money as no need to produce notes and coins.	Administration on paying for small amounts on a card may push costs up.
Shops don't want cash (fear of robbery).	May exclude certain people in society e.g. older generation who are reluctant to embrace technology and vulnerable individuals who may not have access to technology.
Less need for ATMs/high street banks – saves the banks money.	The more we rely on technology, the more we will struggle if it fails.
Many of the reasons for a cashless society benefit businesses more than the individual.	Privacy element of not wanting banks to know exactly what we spend money on.

 DISCUSSION: THE BUDGETING PROCESS **PAGE 41**

Robyn could pay off any outstanding debts, put the surplus in a savings account/ISA, invest the money in shares, give some to charity.

If Robyn's spending was greater than her income, she should look at ways of cutting her spending and research cheaper borrowing options. If she is in financial trouble, she should also speak to the people that she owes money to as they might be able to help with a repayment plan.

DISCUSSION: COMMITTED VS DISCRETIONARY SPENDING PAGE 41

Discussions may focus around whether students consider their smartphone to be a need (committed spending) or want (discretionary spending).

Committed – vital for keeping in contact with people, can't live without it, holds important information and details.

Discretionary – do not have to use a smartphone to communicate with others therefore it is not a need, it is not a necessity, it is a luxury item.

CASE STUDY: MONTHLY BUDGET PAGE 42

INCOME	EXPENDITURE
£1,540 salary	£550 rent
	£65 gas and electricity
	£27.50 water
	£220 shopping (assuming 4 weeks per month)
	£19 subscriptions
	£23.87 insurance
	£240 leisure/going out (assuming 4 weeks per month)
	£34 phone
	£312 travel (assuming 4 weeks per month)
	£90 clothes
	£50 coffee (assuming 4 weeks per month)
TOTAL £1,540	TOTAL £1,631.37

Currently Awurabena is spending more than she earns each month by approximately £92. This also assumes that no other bills come in and that she doesn't overspend on other items (e.g. spending more than £90 on clothes per month).

Therefore, based on her current financial position, she is unable to save for her car. If she is serious about saving for a year, she could:

• Cancel her subscriptions (£19)

• Reduce her leisure/going out budget by half (£120)

• Stop buying clothes and coffee (£140)

This would save her £279 per month and allow her to purchase the car in 12 months and possibly have enough to pay for the insurance too.

DISCUSSION: THE BUDGETING PROCESS PAGE 42

Reasons for having to spend more money may include:

- Additional bills – e.g. school trips, birthday gifts
- Unplanned events – e.g. car/appliance breaks down
- Weather – a cold winter may mean that we spend more on gas/electricity than expected.

Changes that could be made include:

- Cut spending in other areas
- Try to budget (predict) when spending is likely to increase
- Put small, regular amounts in a savings account so money is available if required.

DISCUSSION: KEEPING TRACK OF YOUR BUDGET PAGE 43

Discussions could focus on:

- Exploring the different categories students identity for their spending pots, in addition to those highlighted. This identifies the priorities that different students place on their spending, and will be different for different members of the group
- The way in which different students split the £130 across the pots. This will be different from one student to another. You can explore some of those choices and potentially ask a few students to explain their thought process of their allocation.

ACTIVITY: KEEPING TRACK OF YOUR BUDGET PAGE 44

DATE	TYPE	DESCRIPTION	INCOME	EXPENDITURE	BALANCE
1st July		Opening balance			£26.50
2nd July	CR	Birthday money	£80		£106.50
5th July	DB	Clothes		£35.67	£70.83
6th July	DB	Train ticket		£25.65	£45.18
14th July	CQ	Money for gardening	£20		£65.18
20th July	DB	Food & drink		£12.32	£52.86
21st July	DB	Food & drink		£13.45	£39.41
22nd July	DB	Food & drink		£15.56	£23.85

ACTIVITY: VALUE FOR MONEY PAGE 45

1.

	NUMBER BOUGHT PER WEEK	LUXURY BRAND TOTAL COST	SUPERMARKET OWN BRAND TOTAL COST	VALUE RANGE TOTAL COST
Can of baked beans	4	£4.16	£2.60	£0.92
Cereal	1	£3.65	£2.21	£1.68
Crisps	6	£7.20	£5.94	£2.70
Batteries	2	£7.90	£5.78	£1.98
TOTAL		£22.91	£16.53	£7.28

2a) £22.91 - £16.53 = £6.38   2b) £22.91 - £7.28 = £15.63

	LUXURY BRAND COST PER YEAR	SUPERMARKET OWN BRAND COST PER YEAR	VALUE RANGE COST PER YEAR
Can of baked beans	£216.32	£135.20	£47.84
Cereal	£189.80	£114.92	£87.36
Crisps	£374.40	£308.88	£140.40
Batteries	£410.80	£300.56	£102.96
TOTAL	£1,191.32	£859.56	£378.56

4a) £1,191.32 - £859.56 = £331.76   4b) £1,191.32 - £378.56 = £812.76

 ## ACTIVITY: WHAT'S THE BEST DEAL PAGE 47

CHICKEN	COST PER 100G
200g for £4.50	£2.25
500g for £6.00	£1.20
1kg for £10.00	£1.00 – best deal

EGGS	COST PER EGG
12 for £3.80	0.32p
9 for £2.70	0.30p – best deal
6 for £2.20	0.37p

 ## DISCUSSION: WHAT'S THE BEST DEAL PAGE 47

Discussions may focus on:

- In order to receive a better quality product or service
- Want to receive a product/service straight away
- Getting a better deal for ordering early e.g. pre-ordering games/music
- Get more/additional extras.

ANSWERS:
FURTHER YOUR KNOWLEDGE

OVERSPEND ON BUDGET PAGE 50

INCOME	EXPENDITURE	
Wages as a fitness instructor **£1,200** Fees as a personal trainer **£590**	Rent	**£520**
	Council tax	**£117**
	Gas/electric	**£97**
	Water	**£32**
	Telephone/internet	**£26**
	TV license	**£13**
	Insurance	**£33**
	Credit card balance	**£217**
	Groceries and cleaning materials	**£95**
	Travel	**£62**
	Clothes	**£150**
	Laundry and dry cleaning	**£66**
	Sport activities (inc. football season ticket)	**£104**
	Toiletries and personal grooming	**£68**
	Mobile phone (inc. apps)	**£71**
	Nights out	**£275**
	Other treats (e.g. coffees, computer games)	**£170**
	Presents for other people	**£25**
	Sundries	**£35**
Total income: £1790	Total expenditure: £2176	

VALUE FOR MONEY PAGE 51

1. d (25p per pint)

2. d (£2.10 per kilo)

3. c (£2.45 per kilo)

4. e (11p per egg)

As three of the four items are highly perishable, they are only good deals if they are going to be used before they go off.

CONSUMER RIGHTS **PAGE 52**

	T	F	
You have bought a kettle in a store sale and it is not heating the water. The store tells you that you should complain to the manufacturer.		✓	Clearly the item is faulty and not fit for purpose. As your contract is with the retailer, it is their responsibility to deal with any issues. The fact that it is in a sale is immaterial; sale goods still have to be fit for purpose.
When buying a t-shirt, you have accidentally picked up the wrong size. Your neighbour, who works in the retail sector, tells you that the shop does not have to exchange it.	✓		It is the customer's responsibility to ensure that purchased goods are actually what is wanted. As there is nothing wrong with the manufacture of the t-shirt the shop is within its rights to refuse an exchange. However, many retailers have a refund or exchange policy within a month of purchase, as long as goods are returned in the condition in which they were sold.
You have used your debit card to purchase a pair of trainers but when you get home you find the sole of one of them is coming unstuck. However, you have lost the receipt so that means you won't be able to return them.		✓	The goods are not fit for purpose and having no receipt is not a problem in this case. You will still have "proof of purchase" (which is the legal requirement) because you used a debit card in the transaction, therefore the bank will have a record of the purchase.
You have ordered a necklace online to wear at your 18th birthday party. The agreed delivery date is on the big day, but it actually arrives the day after. You are entitled to a full refund.	✓		If there is an agreed specified delivery date, which is missed, you have a right to a full refund. If a date is not specified, then delivery should be within 30 days. If the arrangement is "click and collect" it is the customer's responsibility to pick up the item in good time.
A book you have been after has turned up in an online auction advertised by a private seller. You buy the book but when it arrives you discover it is one you have already read. However, you are sure you have the same right of return as buying it in a bookstore so it can be sent back to the seller.		✓	Auction purchases are counted as second-hand sales so as long as the seller has not misled you your rights end there. If you bought the wrong book that is your own fault and it is a case of caveat emptor (buyer beware).
The holiday company you are dealing with goes bust and you lose all the hard-earned money you have paid out to it. A friend tells you that you should have used a credit card for this purchase.	✓		You actually have extra protection under Section 75 of the Consumer Credit Act. This protects a consumer paying out between £100 and £30,000 for purchases on a credit card. This makes the card company jointly liable with the retailer, so if something goes wrong, it means you should get your money back.

BORROWING

What does this chapter cover?

This chapter considers why and how young people might want to borrow money and what to do if it proves difficult to repay the debt.

The following topics are explored either through the provision of information and case studies, or through activities for students. Alongside each topic is a possible curriculum link:

TOPIC	CURRICULUM LINK					
	PSHE				CITIZENSHIP	MATHEMATICS
	PLANNING FOR EXPENDITURE	UNDERSTANDING DEBT	BE A CRITICAL CONSUMER	CONSUMER RIGHTS AND REDRESS		
Reasons to borrow	●			●	●	
Good debt and bad debt	●		●		●	
Simple interest	●				●	●
Compound interest	●				●	●
APR			●	●	●	●
Credit history	●	●	●	●	●	●
Methods of borrowing	●	●	●	●	●	
Loan sharks	●	●		●	●	
Manageable and unmanageable debt	●	●		●	●	●

WHY IS THIS TOPIC IMPORTANT FOR YOUNG PEOPLE?

One in five **25-30** year olds use credit to buy day-to-day essentials.

Source: PricewaterhouseCoopers research, 2017

The average interest rate on credit card lending bearing interest was **18.26%** in April 2018.

Source: The Money Charity, June 2018

Citizens Advice Bureau deal with over **4,000** debt problems per day in England and Wales.

Source: The Money Charity, June 2018

28% of young people (aged 25-34) were worried about meeting future debt repayments.

Source: PricewaterhouseCoopers research, 2017

LESSON PLAN BUILDER

Step 1 – Pick a starter activity
(10 – 15 minutes)

Who to borrow from? `PSHE` `CITIZENSHIP`

As you start to teach from the chapter on borrowing, ask students for the names of any companies they have heard on TV who advertise that they can help you with borrowing money. Write student responses on a whiteboard/screen. After a couple of minutes of responses, try to categorise the answers into banks, payday loan companies, credit card providers, etc. Explain that, as you explore the chapter on borrowing, students will begin to understand the pros and cons of these different types of lender, and they will be in a better position to make judgements on the various companies.

What is debt? `PSHE` `CITIZENSHIP`

Before looking at the level of debt in the UK (see page 54), ask students to complete the sentence, "A debt is when …" Then present them with a simple scenario like: Zoe is 15. She and her mates want to see their favourite band, but she hasn't got enough money for the ticket. Josh offers to lend her the money and Zoe says she can pay Josh back after her birthday in two weeks time.

Ask the students – does it still count as debt if you owe money to your friends? You could also extend this to owing money to family – is this debt? Once you have agreed with students what debt is, you could go on to consider the facts about UK debt (see page 54) and discuss whether this figure overestimates debt or underestimates it.

Good debt, bad debt `PSHE` `CITIZENSHIP`

Use the activity on good debt and bad debt (see page 55) – write the six examples on a board/screen at the front of the class and ask students to consider each example in turn and decide whether the borrowing is good or bad. When you have agreed on the answers ask students to suggest another example of a good and bad debt.

Credit card advertisement `PSHE` `CITIZENSHIP` `MATHEMATICS`

Find a typical advertisement from a credit card company – from the internet, a newspaper or one sent to you in the post. Ask students to locate all of the costs associated with that card (some, like late payment fees, may be in the small print). Itemise these costs at the front of the class and discuss with students whether they think everyone who gets a credit card looks at the costs as they have just done.

Interest rates and APR `PSHE` `CITIZENSHIP` `MATHEMATICS`

Before tackling some of the activities on simple and compound interest (see page 58), gather some current examples of APR from bank loans, credit cards, store cards and payday loan companies. Show these to the class and ask them which one is offering the best APR. Once students are clear that a low APR is best, discuss with them why not everyone borrows from the company offering the lowest APR.

Step 2 – Pick a core activity/activities
(25 – 30 minutes)

Making informed choices `PSHE` `CITIZENSHIP`

The case study on Kofi (see page 60) could be answered in a table, which outlines the advantages and disadvantages of his options. As part of the follow-up discussion, ask students to consider whether there are any other options (for example, do not buy the car) and what other costs will Kofi need to consider before making his decision (for example, how much will his insurance be?).

Methods of borrowing `PSHE` `CITIZENSHIP` `MATHEMATICS`

Using the list of forms of borrowing (see page 62), ask students to rank these according to how much interest you pay if you used that form of borrowing. You will need to carry out some preparation to find some common interest rates for each method of borrowing.

Before trying to complete the research activity (see page 64), students could be given some simple scenarios where they must decide which is the most appropriate form of borrowing. For example, a family needs new beds for their two children who have outgrown their old ones. Should they a) buy from a mail order catalogue, b) ask their bank if they can go overdrawn until they can repay the cost of the beds, or c) get a store card for a large department store that sells beds?

Credit cards `PSHE` `CITIZENSHIP`

Use the textbook to explain the nature of credit cards to students (see page 66). Pairs or groups of students could then take on the role of a bank's marketing department, who are asked to create a flyer for a new credit card for potential customers. These customers have either a poor, average, or good credit history. Tell each pair/group who their target customer is.

Ask students to give the card a name and an attractive design, and give it a minimum of five features that they think will make it appealing to their target customers. These features could be: introductory offers/gifts, low interest rate, low penalty fees for late payment, loyalty scheme, etc.

When complete, the pairs can present their cards to the rest of the class and then get the class to vote on which one they think is best. Finish by trying to answer the discussion question about the negatives of having a credit card (see page 67).

Loan sharks `PSHE` `CITIZENSHIP` `MATHEMATICS`

A search of YouTube will reveal a large number of videos that make excellent resources for teaching students about the risks of borrowing from loan sharks. One example is "Loan Sharks", a film produced by the BRANCAB Film Unit for the Illegal Lending Team and Birmingham City Council. This would need to be previewed first and then relevant clips shown to students.

Once students are fully aware of the nature of loan sharks they could use the textbook (see page 70) to compare pay day loan companies and loan sharks. Ask students to compare them in terms of: legality, regulation, interest rates, penalties for non-payment, paperwork needed to get the loan, etc.

Step 3 – Pick an extension activity
(10 – 15 minutes)

Credit unions

Ask students to find out where the nearest credit union is to them and find out if they have any information on borrowing money. For example, how much can you borrow from them, how long can you take to repay the loan, are there any fees to pay when getting a loan, and what rate of interest is charged on the loan? If students go to www.findyourcreditunion.co.uk, they can find the nearest credit union to them by inserting their postcode.

Credit

Students could be asked to find examples of credit deals that are on offer from a range of lenders – credit unions, banks, shop credit deals, payday loan companies – and work out the true cost of borrowing a set amount, say £500 over a year.

They can then present these findings as a blog or web article where they summarise the pros and cons of each credit deal. This could be presented as a table to enable readers to clearly compare each deal.

Impact of changes in interest rates

Discuss with your class the effects of a rise/fall in interest rates on a) an individual b) the economy as a whole.

You can ask students to consider the effects on borrowing, repayments, savings, prices, economic growth and jobs.

Step 4 – Links for further information and extra-curricular opportunities

Extra-curricular opportunities

In addition to the activities identified in the lesson plan builder, there are many opportunities for young people to do work on this topic outside of the curriculum.

Examples include:

- Students research which organisations offer help to those who have got into debt problems.

- Research APRs for different amounts of borrowing, comparing different products (e.g. mortgages, loans, credit cards).

Links

- www.abcul.org
- www.citizensadvice.org.uk
- www.nationaldebtline.org
- www.stepchange.org
- www.stoploansharks.co.uk

ANSWERS:

ACTIVITY: GOOD DEBT, BAD DEBT PAGE 55

- Go on an exotic holiday – Bad

- Buy a car to travel to work each day – Good

- Buy a house to live in – Good

- Get a wardrobe full of new clothes – Bad

- Fund higher education – Good

- Get festival tickets – Bad

ACTIVITY: REPAYING THE DEBT PAGE 57

1. £3,000 x 0.08 x 1 = £240 interest. Total repayment = £3,240

2. £3,000 x 0.225 x 1 = £675 interest. Total repayment = £3,675

3. £3,000 x 0.368 x 1 = £1,104 interest. Total repayment = £4,104

4. £3,000 x 14.99 x 1 = £44,970. Total repayment = £47,970

ACTIVITY: COMPOUND INTEREST FORMULA **PAGE 58**

1. £3,000 x 1.2^2 = £4,320

2. £3,000 x 1.2^4 = £6,220.80

3. £3,000 x 1.2^7 = £10,749.54

4. £3,000 x 1.2^{15} = £46,221.06

5. £3,000 x $1.2^{\frac{1}{2}}$ = £3,286.34

6. £3,000 x $1.2^{\frac{1}{4}}$ = £3,139.91

 ACTIVITY: INTEREST RATES CAN CHANGE **PAGE 58**

1.

- Fixed rate advantage – know exactly how much you will pay each month so helps with budgeting

- Fixed rate disadvantage – you will not benefit if the interest rate falls

- Variable rate advantage – more flexible, so if interest rates fall, so does the repayment

- Variable rate disadvantage – if interest rates rise, so do your repayments.

2.

- A rise in interest rates – pay more interest on the borrowing, may take longer to pay back, lower disposable income, less incentive to save, increase in mortgage repayments

- A fall in interest rates – pay less interest on borrowing, more disposable income, cheaper mortgage repayments, lower return for savers.

3.

- Would not make any difference because the rate is "fixed" at a certain interest rate, so any fluctuations in the interest rate have no impact on borrowing.

 CASE STUDY: FIXED VS VARIABLE RATE **PAGE 58**

1. Option 1, the fixed rate mortgage because you get two years at a reduced, introductory rate.

2.

OPTION 1 – 2 YEAR FIXED	OPTION 2 – VARIABLE RATE
£550.38 x 24 months = £13,209.12 + £709.77 x 276 months = £195,896.52	£696.28 x 300 months =
TOTAL = £209,105.64	TOTAL = £208,884

3. Choose option 2 because it is cheaper by £221.64 over the mortgage term.

4. The interest rate may increase, making repayments more expensive.

5. Yes, option 1 looks cheaper because of the reduced, fixed rate part, but overall it is actually more expensive.

DISCUSSION: APR **PAGE 59**

Discussions could focus around:

- Using representative APRs as a marketing tool to entice people to apply for borrowing

- Even if they don't get the representative APR people may stick with the borrowing product anyway

- Is this ethical if many people do not receive the APR advertised?

CASE STUDY: MAKING INFORMED CHOICES **PAGE 60**

	ADVANTAGES	DISADVANTAGES
Use existing savings	• Can buy the car straight away.	• No savings left for his flat deposit • What about car insurance and other associated driving costs?
Save up	• Satisfaction that he has saved up • He will not have to borrow and get into debt.	• Will take time to save up, so may have to delay purchases of both the car and the flat.
Borrow the money	• Can get the car and flat now.	• Will have to pay back with interest, costing him more money in the long run.

Is there anything further you would like to know before making the final decision?

- What is Kofi's income and expenditure each month?

- Could he cut his spending? Or possibly increase his income?

- Are there any cheaper, alternative ways for Kofi to get to work?

- Could he save more per month?

- Does Kofi have any other debt?

DISCUSSION: HOW BANKS MAKE DECISIONS **PAGE 60**

Discussions could include:

- Income and employment details

- Other borrowing/debt

- Any defaults – previous missed repayments

- Regular monthly outgoings

- Affordability – can they afford the loan repayments?

 ACTIVITY: CREDIT UNIONS V. PAYDAY LENDERS **PAGE 64**

	PROS	CONS
Credit unions	• Not for profit organisations • Provide a secure place to store money • Owned by members and therefore costs can be kept down allowing for higher interest payments on savings and lower rates on borrowing • Often offer additional benefits to the community or a good cause.	• Not available in all areas of the UK • May lack some of the features of a commercial bank (e.g. online banking).
Payday lenders	• May be suitable in an emergency to meet an immediate cash flow problem • Easy to access.	• Interest rates are very high • The final sum owed can be much higher than the initial amount borrowed • The cumulative amount owed can quickly spiral out of control.

CASE STUDY: PERSONAL LOANS PAGE 65

1. Despite all having the same APR, the 1 year loan is the cheapest but does mean that the monthly payments are more expensive. Even though the 3 year loan looks more attractive as the monthly repayments seem quite cheap, Paige would be paying much more interest over the term of the loan.

2.

• Do you really need a loan?

• Are you sure this is the bike you want?

• Do you need to borrow £1,000?

• Can you afford the repayments?

• Can anyone else help you to buy it?

• What happens if you can't pay it off?

• What plans would you have in place if you lost your job or couldn't afford the repayments?

3.

Paige could get a credit card which may be cheaper than a loan as they sometimes offer 0% interest rates for an introductory period. She would still have to make monthly payments and she would need to make sure that she doesn't use the card to purchase other goods/services as this will increase her repayments.

She could also borrow from a family member.

4. No – Paige could save up her wages and delay purchasing the bike straight away. She may also be able to save money that she receives as a gift (e.g. birthday money). She also could work more hours to increase her income.

If she budgets to save £100 per month, she could raise £1,000 in 10 months which is shorter than repaying the 1 year loan with interest.

DISCUSSION: CREDIT CARDS PAGE 67

Discussions could include:

• Interest is charged on balances not paid off within a month

• Too convenient and can encourage customer to overspend and get into debt

• Higher interest is charged on cash withdrawals

• Missed payments may result in a poor credit history, so may be unable to borrow in the future

• If you only repay the minimum amount, it will take a long time to pay off the debt and will accrue significant interest over time.

CASE STUDY: CREDIT CARDS PAGE 67

1. People who have a good credit history are more likely to receive more favourable interest rates. This is because they have previously proven that they are able to repay on time.

People who have never applied for credit or have been unable to repay the debt are less likely to get preferential rates. This is because the bank does not know whether the person will be able to meet the repayments (as they have never had credit before) or they have previously been a risk.

- Yes, it's fair – the bank is protecting their profit

- People who are good at repaying should receive a more favourable rate

- Everyone's circumstances are different, so everyone's interest rates should reflect their ability to repay

- No, it's not fair – everyone should have the same rate.

2.
- Pay all bills on time, do not miss payments

- Pay off the debt – don't keep moving it around to different credit cards

- Pay any outstanding debt before applying for new credit

- Check their credit report to make sure their details are accurate; even a wrong address can impact their score

- Get help if they are having problems meeting the repayments – don't avoid it.

3.
- Consider the cheapest forms of borrowing before you apply and, even better, save up so you don't need to take out credit!

- Always pay your bills on time as this may reduce your APR.

- Never use all available credit.

- Always try to pay off your credit card in total at the end of each month. If this isn't possible, pay as much as you have available.

- Always pay your credit card bill on time by setting up a direct debit, this will mean that you never miss a repayment.

- Shop around for the best deal before you apply. Many companies offer introductory 0% interest rates for up to 36 months, but always remember to move your credit card once this rate is over as you will then move onto a standard rate.

CASE STUDY: PAYDAY LENDERS **PAGE 69**

1. No, Amelia doesn't have the level of income to be able to pay all of her bills and the outstanding loans in six months.

2.

- The experience affects her ability to access credit in the future if she is unable to pay

- It may put her off dealing with financial institutions in the future.

Amelia may feel:

- Anxious and upset about how she has ended up in so much debt

- Ashamed and embarrassed about her financial situation

- Worried about how she will make the repayments.

3.

- No, they should not allow Amelia access to further credit until she is able to pay off the original debt

- The payday lender should undertake more checks to ensure the person borrowing the money is able to pay back the loan

- They should not be sending her emails encouraging her to spend more as they know that she is struggling to meet the repayments.

4.

- Get impartial financial advice from either the Money Advice Service or Citizens Advice

- Talk to her bank to see if they can offer any support

- Consider moving back into her parents' house until she is able to afford living independently

- Do not take out any further loans with the company.

5.

- Consolidate the debt by getting a loan that can be paid off over the longer term and will probably have a lower interest rate than the payday lender

- See if a family member can help her out and lend her the money.

ANSWERS:
FURTHER YOUR KNOWLEDGE

MORTGAGE BORROWING PAGE 72

1. The amount of interest charged each year is reducing over time and, in contrast, the amount of principal being repaid each year is increasing over time. As the remaining balance of the principal is reduced, this in turn reduces the interest charged.

2. The average monthly interest payment on the mortgage is £145.40 (over 25 years there are 300 months.) **The total interest is £43,621.23. £43,621.23/300 = £145.40**

3. Example:

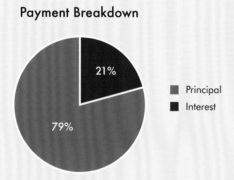

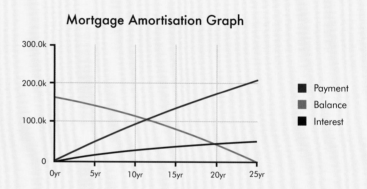

HIGH COST CREDIT PAGE 73

A list of 10 bullet points detailing the main points set out in the speech could include:

- Types of high cost credit
- Focus areas e.g. credit cards and payday lenders
- How many adults have used high cost credit
- Who is most likely to use it

- Why it is used
- Amount of outstanding debt
- What are the alternatives

MAKING BORROWING CHOICES PAGE 73

Toni

	MONTHLY REPAYMENT	TOTAL INTEREST	TOTAL COST OF LOAN
a)	£40.97	£41.65	£491.65
b)	£39.85	£28.24	£478.24
c)	£42.77	£63.24	£523.24

If Toni chooses options a) or c) she will be able to buy the console more or less immediately as they are both forms of pre-authorised credit. What might initially look like a small difference between the monthly repayments for these options becomes more apparent in the totals columns. The reward points for option c) may be significant but may also tempt her into further spending.

Option b) is the cheapest but she will need to apply and wait for confirmation of the loan which could mean losing the sale deal. If Toni has some money set aside, does she need to borrow the full amount? Could a family member loan her the money at a cheaper rate? Could she delay her gratification…by which time an even newer and more expensive model may have caught her eye?

Dane

	MONTHLY REPAYMENT	TOTAL INTEREST	TOTAL COST OF LOAN
a)	£25.51	£418.19	£918.19
b)	£330.45	£1,482.68	£1982.68
c)	£500	£8,500.03	£9,000.03

Dane is in a poor position to borrow money but really does have a need for the washer/dryer; using a laundrette will cost even more. There is a huge risk in borrowing from an unregulated loan shark (option c) and he will end up paying back 18 times the cost of the machine – even if the first three months provide a breathing space. He would not be able to make the monthly payments for option b) either so would probably incur further interest charges as well as administration fees when he cannot make a payment.

Dane can just about afford the monthly repayments for option a), although he will still end up paying significantly more than the actual cost of the machine. The interest-free option from the internet catalogue might help but he has to be sure he can pay the full amount by, or before, the due date to avoid further penalties and charges.

Dane should check that he is claiming all benefits to which he is entitled and might consider applying for a budgeting loan or budgeting advance from the social fund (**www.moneyadviceservice.org.uk/en/articles/budgeting-loans-and-budgeting-advances**).

Citizens Advice may be able to advise him further. Finally, he should check his credit rating before applying for any further loans/credit.

Faisal

	MONTHLY REPAYMENT	TOTAL INTEREST	TOTAL COST OF LOAN
a)	£121.96	£890.56	£4,390.56
b)	£111.85	£526.20	£4,026.20
c)	£110	£975	£4,475

The dealership loan might be the most convenient to arrange but still slightly exceeds the amount that Faisal can afford each month. He must also remember that the TV does not legally belong to him until the agreement is paid off in full.

The bank loan is the cheapest option but needs organising separately before he can buy the TV, and the monthly repayment still slightly exceeds the budgeted amount. While the credit card can be paid off with the budgeted amount each month it will actually take 3 years and 5 months to do so; the accrued interest is also significantly higher.

On balance, option b) provides the best fit. Alternatively, he might need to consider waiting until his income rises. Faisal also needs to consider the cost of a TV licence, subscriptions to streaming services, and the possibility that he may want new supplementary equipment (e.g. new surround sound speakers)?

MOVING ON FROM SCHOOL – THE WORLD OF WORK

What does this chapter cover?

This chapter considers the financial matters and decisions that young people face as they move on from full-time education.

The following topics are explored either through the provision of information and case studies, or through activities for students. Alongside each topic is a possible curriculum link:

TOPIC	CURRICULUM LINK					
	PSHE				CITIZENSHIP	MATHEMATICS
	CHANGING PATTERNS OF EMPLOYMENT	MANAGING RISK	PLANNING FOR EXPENDITURE	CONSUMER RIGHTS AND REDRESS		
Possible next steps after school	X		X		X	
Student tuition fees and student loans				X	X	
Student bursaries				X	X	
Budgeting as a student			X		X	X
Payslip terminology					X	X
How to calculate Income Tax payments					X	X
How to calculate National Insurance payments					X	X
Self-employed	X	X			X	X
The history of Income Tax					X	
Types of pension		X		X	X	X
The ageing UK population					X	X
National Minimum Wage and National Living Wage				X	X	
Welfare system					X	
Methods of payment					X	X

WHY IS THIS TOPIC IMPORTANT FOR YOUNG PEOPLE?

In the first **3** months of 2018, **the unemployment rate of young people aged 16-24** who were not in full-time education was **10%**

Source: House of Commons briefing paper number 5871

51% of **14-17 year-olds** could not identify pension contributions correctly from a payslip, and **62%** could not identify how much had been paid.

Source: Money Advice Service – Young Adults and Money Management: behaviours, attitudes and useful rules of thumb, January 2018

44% of 18-34-year-olds say they have **no pension provision** whatsoever.

Source: Bridging the Young Adults Pension Gap, YouGov 2017

1 IN 3 youngsters in England were **awarded university places** in **2017**

Source: www.independent.co.uk Sunday 17 September 2017

LESSON PLAN BUILDER

Step 1 – Pick a starter activity
(10 – 15 minutes)

Pay and payslip terminology `PSHE` `CITIZENSHIP`

Before starting any work on payslips, and in particular the payslip for Sam Green (see page 82), use a starter to see what the students' current knowledge is of the terminology associated with payslips. Examples of the terminology include: gross pay, net pay, Income Tax, National Insurance, BACS, deductions, take-home pay, tax code, pension, employer and employee. One approach for a starter activity is to use some, or all, of the above and put them into a word search using one of the many word search generators that are available online.

Alternatively, you could choose some or all of these and make anagrams of them for students to find the correct word or term. In both examples, you could set a target, of say six, and stop when one student reaches the target. Then, work on the payslip and go through the answers to the ones they did not get at the end of the lesson when you will have explained what each term means.

Payment sources `PSHE` `CITIZENSHIP`

Using the methods of payment and their definitions (see page 88), think of some jobs that could be paid by the different methods. Put this list of jobs at the front and ask students to match the methods of payment to the job. Examples could be: a shop assistant in a department store (commission); a teacher (salary); a hotel cleaner (wages) an accountant who checks the accounts for a small business (fees).

You could provide examples for all of the methods of payment or just keep it limited to five or six, as some jobs could well be paid using more than one method (e.g. a sales representative who gets a basic salary and a bonus for reaching their target).

Celebrity salary levels PSHE CITIZENSHIP MATHEMATICS

Students will be interested in the levels of pay earned by celebrities. A search of the internet or publications like the The Sunday Times Rich List can be used to identify 10 celebrities and how much they earn. Mix up the names and the pay levels and see if students can match the celebrity to how much they earn.

This could be used as a starter for work on payslips or it could be combined with the extension activity on average salaries in step 3.

Videos PSHE CITIZENSHIP

Before any work on the aging population and pensions (see page 92), it would be useful to see what student attitudes are towards pensions. Begin by simply asking for a show of hands to see which students have: a) heard of pensions; b) understand what they are c) think they are relevant to them.

Trying to convince young people that pensions are relevant and that they need to start saving into a pension scheme can be very difficult – it is very easy to put it off and pensions are not always well understood. Some pension providers have produced some short snappy videos to try and get the attention of young people. You could use the link below to show how one pension provider tries to get the message across.

https://www.aviva.co.uk/retirement/shape-my-future/unlock-my-future/video/time-reality-check/
After you have watched the advert, briefly discuss whether this would alter student attitudes towards pensions.

Price of essentials PSHE CITIZENSHIP MATHEMATICS

The case study on Syrah (see page 80) will initiate a lot of discussion over how much she is spending each week on food, drink and other expenses. Before starting the case study, check to see the students' understanding of day-to-day expenses. One method is to organise a short test to see if students know the price of 6-10 essential items like toilet paper, milk, bread and coffee etc. Research the prices yourself first using either a supermarket website or a price comparison website.

Step 2 – Pick a core activity/activities
(25 – 30 minutes)

Payslips CITIZENSHIP MATHEMATICS

The payslip for Sam Green (see page 82) would be best shown on a whiteboard and left on show as you explain the various elements of it to the class. Expect a lot of discussion from the students who will be very interested in this.

Complete the worked examples of Income Tax (see page 83) with the class before asking students to complete the activity on working out tax (see page 84).

Methods of payment case studies CITIZENSHIP MATHEMATICS

The case studies on Alba and Tyrell (see page 88) and Tom and Lisa (see page 89) could be done individually or in pairs. For the case study on Tom and Lisa, you could give the class large cards with T on one side and L on the other. Once they have written/discussed their answer with their partner, ask them to show either a T(om) or L(isa) depending on who they think has the best pay deal. Then collate the reasons given on a whiteboard/computer. To give an additional maths element to this, you could ask students to calculate at what level of sales does Tom's income fall below Lisa's next year (answer £739,999).

The question on the case study about Alba and Tyrell could again be done individually or in pairs with students deciding which of the two has the best job and ranking the five differences in order of importance (for the job they have chosen as best).

Student finance PSHE CITIZENSHIP

This is a good opportunity to explore the financial impact of going to university. However, it is important to maintain balance as some of the costs can appear daunting to students. One way of maintaining this balance is to get students to complete a table showing the costs and benefits of going to university. Start this before explaining fees, loans and bursaries (see pages 79 to 81) and add to it as new suggestions come forward.

Create two columns – one for costs, one for benefits – and create two rows, one for financial and the other non-financial. Examples could be: **financial costs** – loans to pay back, using up savings; **financial benefits** – better job chances when qualified, loans only have to be repaid when earnings reach a certain level; **non-financial costs** – lose touch with friends from home, leaving the family home; **non-financial benefits** – better social activities, living independently. These are only suggestions.

When all the financial terms have been explained and the table is complete, take the opportunity to explain to students that they will need to weigh up the costs and benefits – financial and non-financial when they make their decision whether or not to go to university.

Living away from home PSHE CITIZENSHIP MATHEMATICS

The case study giving details of Syrah's spending habits as a first-year student is a good route into the idea of preparing budgets (see page 80). Read the case study and answer the follow-up questions, which involve drawing up a budget for Syrah and giving advice on areas of spending she should reduce and whether she should look for extra income.

This is also a good opportunity to consider what Syrah needs to spend money on and what she wants to spend money on. Students could also draw up a table comparing living away from home to living at home. In maths lessons you could take the opportunity to do work on number, graphs and ratios when using these figures.

The ageing population and pensions `CITIZENSHIP` `MATHEMATICS`

The activity and questions about the ageing population (see page 92) could be combined with some work on explaining the different types of pension. The information section on pensions (see page 91) could be read to the class by you, or read in pairs/groups, with you following up with questions like the ones provided in the textbook (see page 92). There is the opportunity to show the trends graphically and you could discuss what life expectancy might be when the students reach retirement age.

The case study on the average pensioner (see page 93) gives an opportunity to consider whether a state pension alone is enough to live on and to analyse the spending of a typical pensioner. Students could be asked to consider how this might differ from a student at university and how it may change over time.

Step 3 – Pick an extension activity

(10 – 15 minutes)

Average salaries

Students could carry out some research on the internet and see if they can find the average salary for at least five of the following jobs: army sergeant, doctor, electrician, lawyer, MP, police constable, plumber, receptionist, vet, and vicar. They can add other jobs, especially ones they are interested in.

Students could write the title of the job on one piece of paper or card and write the average salary on another. Then mix the paper/cards up and see if classmates/family/friends can match the salary to the job.

Successful school leavers

Going straight from school into full-time employment is difficult to do, but for many who do not want to commit to a specific apprenticeship or a degree course at university, this is the route to take. The following all left school to go straight into employment: Simon Cowell, Richard Branson, Joss Stone, Jodie Kidd, Alan Sugar, Chris Evans and former Prime Minister, John Major.

Students could research the internet to see if they can find another successful individual who left school early with very few qualifications. Then try to identify what qualities/skills they have/had that made them succeed in their jobs without having succeeded at school.

Types of apprenticeship

Direct students to **https://www.gov.uk/government/publications/a-guide-to-apprenticeships** and try to find a list of the different types of apprenticeships in the A to Z of apprenticeships. They could identify three apprenticeships that they think might suit their skills and interests and report back to their friends/classmates.

Step 4 – Links for further information and extra-curricular opportunities

Extra-curricular opportunities

In addition to the activities identified above, there are many opportunities for young people to do work on this topic outside of the curriculum.

Examples include:

- Talk to other family members about their own understanding of tax and National Insurance

- Visit the website of a university or college near to them and see if they can find out what extra financial help they provide for students

- Start their own research on what qualifications are needed to do courses at university they are interested in

- Ask elderly family members what advice they would give about pensions.

Links

- www.gov.uk
- www.livingwage.org.uk
- www.ucas.com
- www.moneysavingexpert.com
- www.acas.org.uk
- www.yougov.co.uk

ANSWERS:

ACTIVITY: APPRENTICESHIPS PAGE 76

1. £129.50 per week

2. Income Tax, National Insurance, pension contributions

ACTIVITY: MINIMUM WAGE PAGE 78

1. £206.50 for 19-year-old and £274.05 for 28-year-old

2. £10,738 for 19-year-old and £14,250.60 for 28-year-old

ACTIVITY: GOING TO UNIVERSITY PAGE 78

1. £27,750 (3 x £9,250)

2. £230 per week x 40 = £9,200 per year. 3 years = £27,600

DISCUSSION: STUDENT LOANS PAGE 80

Discussions may focus on:

- They are a graduate tax because the repayments work much like Income Tax and National Insurance. You repay 9% of your income above £25,000 a year e.g. if your income is £28,000 your yearly student loan repayments would be £270 (£28,000 income – £25,000 threshold = £3,000 and 9% of £3,000 = £270)

- They have very specific terms and conditions which are not like traditional borrowing

  o They do not form part of your credit history or report

  o Repayments are taken from your salary (like Income Tax)

  o After 30 years debt is cancelled

- They are a loan because you are borrowing the money in order to fund university education which needs to be paid back.

CASE STUDY: BUDGETING AT UNIVERSITY **PAGE 80**

1. After paying her rent (£1,440) and the amount she has already spent (£507), Syrah has £933 to last her 9 more weeks which is approximately £103 per week.

Her weekly budget might look like:

• Food and drink	£30
• Transport	£10
• Mobile	£10
• Books	£10
• Insurance	£13
• Socialising	£30
TOTAL	**£103**

Total spending over 3 weeks = £507, so average spending for 1 week = £169. If the term is 12 weeks and she maintained her spending habits, her total spending would be £169 x 12 = £2,028.

She has also paid her rent which was £1,440 so her total spending could be £3,468.

As she only gets £2,880 maintenance loan this means she is likely to be in debt by approximately £588 if she doesn't reduce her spending.

2.
- She needs to stop buying clothes and cancel her gym membership
- Walk to uni, if possible, to reduce her transport costs
- Take her washing home rather than use a laundry (if possible)
- Reduce her socialising and food bills
- Spread her book costs over the terms.

 DISCUSSION: PAYSLIPS **PAGE 82**

- Income Tax
- National Insurance
- Financial year starts in April (which is month 1) so June is month 3

- It is the amount of Personal Tax Allowance that you get per year. 1185L means that you get a tax-free allowance of £11,850 before you start paying income tax.
- £1,347.89

 ACTIVITY: INCOME TAX **PAGE 84**

1. None (salary is below the threshold)

2.

Income (£)	Tax rate (%)	Tax paid (£)
11,850	0	0
34,500	20	6,900
20,500	40	8,200
Total 55,000		15,100

Note: These are the figures for England. Scotland has different Income Tax bands.

3.

Income (£)	Tax rate (%)	Tax paid (£)
11,850	0	0
34,500	20	6,900
48,500	40	19,400
Total 83,000		26,300

ACTIVITY: NATIONAL INSURANCE **PAGE 85**

£10,000 per year – On the first £8,424 of their salary National Insurance is zero
They pay 12% on the remaining £1,576 of their salary = £189.12 per year (or £15.76 per month).
They do not earn enough to reach the upper threshold

£30,000 per year – On the first £8,424 of their salary National Insurance is zero
They pay 12% on the remaining £21,576 of their salary = £2,589.12 per year (or £215.76 per month).
They do not earn enough to reach the upper threshold

£100,000 per year – On the first £8,424 of their salary National Insurance is zero
They pay 12% on the next £37,926 of their salary = £4,551 per year
They pay 2% on the final £53,650 of their salary = £1,073 per year
So, in total, the lawyer pays £4,551 + £1,073 = £5,624 per year (or £469 per month)

ACTIVITY: SELF-EMPLOYMENT **PAGE 87**

1.

	Profit (£)	Tax rate (%)	Tax paid (£)
	11,850	0	0
	16,150	20	3,230
Total	28,000		3,230

Note: These are the figures for England. Scotland has different tax bands.

2. £48,000 profit per year – Class 2 National Insurance – £2.95 x 52 (weeks in a year) = £153.40
Plus, Class 4 National Insurance – on first £8,424 of profits, National Insurance is £0
Then pay 9% on next £37,926 of profits = £3,413.34
Then pay 2% on final £1,650 of profits = £33
Total National Insurance = £153.40 + £3,413.34 + £33 = £3,599.74 per year

CASE STUDY: METHODS OF PAYMENTS **PAGE 88**

- Alba is self-employed and Tyrell is an employee of a company

- Alba can take time off when she wants to and Tyrell would have to have his holidays approved in advance

- Tyrell is guaranteed an income and Alba will only get paid if she completes a job

- Alba has the opportunity of expanding her business and earning more money whilst Tyrell does not have this option

- Tyrell gets holiday pay and Alba does not get paid if she goes on holiday

- Tyrell gets double time if he works above and beyond his contracted hours whilst Alba does not.

CASE STUDY: METHODS OF PAYMENT **PAGE 89**

Tom's income last year would total £40,000 (£15,000 salary, plus £25,000 commission). Last year Lisa would have received the most income.

Next year, Tom's income would increase to £55,000 (£15,000 salary plus £40,000 commission). In this case, Tom would receive the most income, so long as he meets his target. However, if Tom misses his target this could change.

 ACTIVITY: WHAT HAPPENS TO OUR TAXES? **PAGE 90**

1. Students may identify the below:
- Income Tax and National insurance – through earnings
- Excise duties – if you buy petrol, alcohol and tobacco
- VAT – buying most goods and services (20%)
- Council tax – based on property values
- If they have own business – you may pay business rates and corporation tax (tax on business profits).

2. Positive effects of tax
- Contributing to services that you use day-to-day (e.g. health, education, welfare, street lighting)
- We all have a social responsibility to support the state
- Lower taxes increase economic growth, businesses can supply more, increases employment, consumers have more money to spend, demand for products increases.

3. Negative effects of tax
- Money is taken from your income reducing the amount you have to spend
- Spending less reduces the demand for products and services which may mean they increase in price.

4. The areas which receive the most funding:
- Social protection – this is the welfare budget and is the payment of benefits to individuals
- Health – including NHS
- Education – funding for schools and colleges.

5. Yes, it means that the government is spending more than it gains in revenue; in other words, the country is in national debt which means there may be increased taxes to reduce the deficit.

6. Yes, tax is a good thing:
- Raises revenue for government
- Discourages over consumption
- Controls pollution
- Equality of income
- Controls demand.

No, tax is not a good thing:
- Contributes to inflation (price rises)
- Incentive to work lost
- Tax avoidance
- Reliance on welfare
- May lead to higher unemployment.

ACTIVITY: AGEING POPULATION **PAGE 92**

1. Men and women are living longer, women are living longer than men.

2. People are working longer.

3.

- The government – as we live longer, we are likely to receive pensions for longer, making state pension payments at their current level unaffordable for the government unless action is taken. The government is increasing state pension ages to try to bring this cost under control.

- People who are working – people have to work longer until they receive their state pension.

- People who are retired – living longer on less income.

 ## CASE STUDY: PENSIONS **PAGE 93**

Current full state pension is £160 per week, that's £8,320 per year and falls short of the minimum UK living costs of £10,850 per year.

Advice:
- Have additional savings/investments
- Reduce discretionary spending
- Take out a workplace pension (at the beginning of a career, if possible).

 ## ACTIVITY: NATIONAL MINIMUM WAGE **PAGE 94**

Current National Minimum Wage – if you are under 18 – £4.20 per hour, aged 18-20 – £5.90 per hour, and aged 21-24 – £7.38 per hour

Current National Living Wage is £7.83 per hour

Current UK Voluntary Living Wage is £8.75 per hour (£10.20 per hour London rate)

The government has not made the National Living Wage the same as the Voluntary Living Wage as it will cost too much for businesses to implement. If businesses have to pay more in wages, this may result in an increase in prices (i.e. inflation).

ANSWERS:
FURTHER YOUR KNOWLEDGE

TAX BANDS PAGE 96

1. Jamie's current income is:

£25,350 + (3 x £3,250 = £9,750) + £8,875 = **£43,975**

INCOME (£)	TAX RATE (%)	TAX PAID (£)
11,850	0	0
32,125	20	**6,425**
43,975		

Jamie will pay **£6,425** income tax

2. £43,975 – £6,425 = £37,550 per year

£37,550 / 12 = **£3,129.17 per month**

3. £6,450 / £43,975 x 100 = **14.6%** – This means that 14.6% of Jamie's salary is paid to HMRC in Income Tax.

4.

INCOME (£)	TAX RATE (%)	TAX PAID (£)
11,850	0	0
34,500	20	6,900
2,625	40	1,050
48.975		**7,950**

Jamie will now pay **£7,950** Income Tax

5. £7,950 / £48,975 x 100 = **16.2%** – This means that 16.2% of Jamie's salary is paid to HMRC in Income Tax.

6. Income Tax on £48,975 = £7,950

Income Tax on £43,975 = £6,425 = **£1,525**

7.

- A higher proportion of her earnings is now paid in income tax
- The bonus payment will push Jamie into the 40% higher tax band
- All additional earnings will now be charged at the 40% tax band
- The bonus isn't as lucrative as perhaps it originally seemed

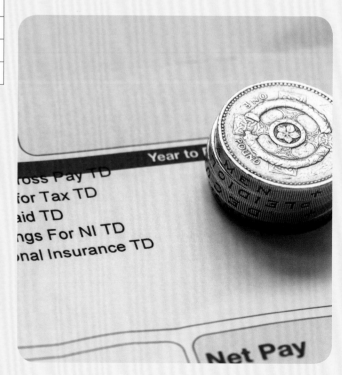

PENSION CONTRIBUTIONS **PAGE 96**

Question 1

a)

EMPLOYER PAYS	EMPLOYEE PAYS
3% – £720 per year (£60 per month)	5% – £1,200 per year (£100 per month)

b)

EMPLOYER PAYS	EMPLOYEE PAY
6% – £1,440 per year (£120 per month)	8% – £1,920 per year (£160 per month)

c) While you would hope that this is the case it is not guaranteed. The contributions both employer and employee make into a pension are managed by a pension provider who invests this in portfolio of investments. The growth of an individual's pension fund depends on the performance of these investments.

Question 2

a)

  i. £16,120

  ii. £32,500

  iii. £68,750

SALARY	EMPLOYEE CONTRIBUTION	EMPLOYER CONTRIBUTION
£16,120	£1,773.20 per year (£147.77 per month)	£2,305.16 per year (£192.10 per month)
£32,500	£4,192.50 per year (£349.38 per month)	£4,647.50 per year (£387.30 per month)
£68,750	£9,281.25 per year (£773.44 per month)	£9,831.25 per year (£819.27 per month)

b) Suggested answers may include:

- Yes – those that earn more should pay more

- No – there should be more increments at more regular intervals, what if you wanted to pay more, or less, as an employee?

SELF-EMPLOYMENT **PAGE 97**

a)

MONTH	HOURS WORKED	INCOME (£30 PER HOUR)	EXPENSES (£)	PROFIT/LOSS
April	168	5,040	927	4,113
May	195	5,850	1,621	4,229
June	110	3,300	782	2,518
July	72	2,160	437	1,723
August	46	1,380	210	1,170
September	197	5,910	2,932	2,978
TOTAL	**788**	**23,640**	**6,909**	**16,731**

b)

PROFIT (£)	TAX RATE (%)	TAX PAID (£)
11,850	0	0
4,881	20	**976.20**
16,731		

RISK AND REWARD

What does this chapter cover?

This chapter considers when and why young people might want to take a financial risk and what the consequences may be if the risk turns out to be a good decision, or a bad decision.

The following topics are explored either through the provision of information and case studies, or through activities for students. Alongside each topic is a possible curriculum link:

TOPIC	CURRICULUM LINK					
	PSHE				CITIZENSHIP	MATHEMATICS
	MANAGING RISK	PLANNING FOR EXPENDITURE	BEING A CRITICAL CONSUMER	CONSUMER RIGHTS AND REDRESS		
Types of personal financial risk	X		X		X	
Weighing up risk	X		X		X	X
Attitudes to risk	X				X	X
Types of investment	X	X	X		X	X
Gambling	X				X	
Types of reward	X	X	X		X	
Negative consequences of taking risks	X				X	X
How to protect against financial risk	X			X	X	
Types of insurance	X				X	

WHY IS THIS TOPIC IMPORTANT FOR YOUNG PEOPLE?

About **40%** of young people go abroad **without travel insurance**, risking medical fees of thousands of pounds if they are taken ill.

Source: Association of British Travel Agents (ABTA) survey 2017

18-24 year-olds are **most likely to be prompted to gamble** by adverts and posts on social media.

Source: Gambling commission annual report, February 2018

LESSON PLAN BUILDER

Step 1 – Pick a starter activity

(10 – 15 minutes)

Assets   PSHE   CITIZENSHIP

As a starter to work on types of personal financial risk (see page 100), ask students to list their three most valuable assets. Compare answers from the class then follow up with the question on the three most valuable assets someone might own over their lifetime (see page 101).

Sports with risk   PSHE   CITIZENSHIP   MATHEMATICS

Before they start the activities on weighing up risk (see page 102), ask for a volunteer to come to the front of the class. Show them the name of a sport with a high level of risk but don't let the rest of the class know what it is. The class must then try to guess what the sport is by asking the student "yes" or "no" questions.

Limit the class to a certain number of questions (e.g. five or six) before they must guess the answer – possibly one question per group. Examples could include: boxing, mountaineering, rugby, horse riding and ice hockey. If time permits, ask the class to rank the sports in order by weighing up the risk in each.

Exchange rates   PSHE   CITIZENSHIP   MATHEMATICS

A starter activity on exchange rates will help students to see that different groups will gain or lose by a rise or fall in the exchange rate. This can be used when doing work on investments (see page 104). Using the current euro exchange rate and some historical data, create some simple exercises to show how changing exchange rates affect different groups. For example: "Today the exchange rate is... This time last year it was... If you went on holiday to Spain and had saved up £500 in spending money would you have had more to spend last year or now?" Then, using the same exchange rates: "A British chocolate manufacturer sells its bars of chocolate (£1 a bar in the UK) to Spanish shops. Do you think they would sell more at last year's exchange rate or this year's?"

Gambling – heads and tails   PSHE   CITIZENSHIP   MATHEMATICS

Ask all students to stand up and either put their hands on their heads or behind their back. Toss a coin, if it is heads all those who had their hands on the heads stay standing all the others sit down, the opposite if it is tails. Repeat the exercise until you have just one person left standing.

Use this as an introduction to any work on gambling (see page 106). You might want to have a prize for the winner but use the exercise to point out how many students lost. Students could look at the probability of being the winner and compare it to the odds of winning the lottery (see page 106).

Spreading the risks `PSHE` `CITIZENSHIP`

Write the 10 financial phrases (see page 111) on separate pieces of card and distribute among pairs of students. At random, ask pairs to try and explain the phrase that they have been given. Ask students if they know of any others that are not on the cards.

Step 2 – Pick a core activity/activities
(25 – 30 minutes)

Weighing up risk `PSHE` `CITIZENSHIP`

Follow the starter for this section of work by completing the activity on comparing attitudes to risk (see page 102). Then, move on from general attitudes to risk by asking students to think about risk in a financial situation. Do this by giving students some financial situations and ask them to identify whether it is a low, medium or high-risk activity and what the advantages and disadvantages of each would be.

Examples of these situations could be:

- Keeping your money in a bank or building society savings account
- Borrowing money from the bank to buy a second-hand car from a friend of a friend
- Booking an expensive holiday with a little-known or unregistered travel company
- You are busy at work, so you give a colleague your debit card and PIN (Personal Identification Number) to get money out of the cash machine for you
- Getting a credit card.

Students could be asked to consider just one of the situations – allocate a different situation to different pairs/ small groups of students, then collate the answers at the front of the class. Follow it up with the activity on drawing a timeline (see page 103).

Types of investment `PSHE` `CITIZENSHIP` `MATHEMATICS`

Explain the different types of investment to students (see page 104). Use the follow-up questions and activities on investment to consolidate the learning. The case study of Sandeep and Noor (see page 108) could be done individually or in pairs but give plenty of time for discussion over share prices and cryptocurrencies.

Gambling `PSHE` `CITIZENSHIP` `MATHEMATICS`

This is an area that students will be interested in exploring. Following the starter and explanation of the different types of gambling (see page 106), ask students to create a mind map of words/phrases to do with gambling. Collect some responses from the class.

To explore student attitudes to gambling, they could create a survey with a series of bold statements about gambling and ask people completing the survey to give a number from 1 to 5 where 1 = strongly agree; 2 = agree; 3 = not sure; 4 = disagree; 5 = strongly disagree. The results of the survey can then be analysed and represented in a variety of ways e.g. using spreadsheets to create graphs and charts.

Insurance `PSHE` `CITIZENSHIP`

Insurance is a term that most students will have heard but a significant number will not know how it works. The worked example of the holiday to Spain (see page 111) should be explained to the class. Refer to the statistic on young people and holiday insurance at the start of this chapter in the teacher's guide. A search of the internet will reveal a number of case studies of young people who did not have insurance and then fell ill while abroad.

The table of types of insurance and what is covered (see page 112) lends itself to being adapted as a card sort. Follow up each type of insurance with an example. The spidergram activity (see page 114) and the case study of Emil and Aliyah (see page 114) can be done in pairs or individually.

Rewards `PSHE` `CITIZENSHIP` `MATHEMATICS`

Create a share game to use when explaining the different types of reward (see page 108). Select up to 10 well-known companies from a range of sectors that students will be aware of and find their share price currently and what it was a year ago. Tell students the share price from one year ago and explain that they have inherited £1000 (or an amount of your choice). You could add a brief description of each company and how it has performed in previous years. They must now decide what to do with the £1000. They can invest some, all or none of their money. Remind students of the work done previously on spreading the risk (see page 110). Any money not invested will earn 1% interest over the year. The exercise will be best done in pairs or small groups.

An alternative approach would be to get the students to do all of the research in groups and challenge another group to invest in the companies they have gathered data on. You will need to ensure that different groups have different companies and might want to restrict it to just five companies per group.

When they have made their decision, reveal the current share price – one company at a time. Ask if anyone invested in that company, give the new share price and get them to work out their gain/loss. Some pairs/groups will do better than others, use the plenary to refer to the other types of investment like unit trusts and property (see page 104).

Step 3 – Pick an extension activity
(10 – 15 minutes)

Attitudes to risk

Ask students to devise a survey to assess other students' attitude to risk. It could follow a similar format to that suggested for the gambling survey. Online research will provide some examples of questions to ask, but students may also wish to add their own. For example, on smoking, drugs, sports, homework and relationships – while keeping the questions inoffensive and nonintrusive.

Share game

The share game above could easily be extended over a longer period. Devise your own rules around how often they can change companies as in other "fantasy" competitions. For example, a Friday transfer day when students are allowed to make three changes.

Gambling

There are many readily available resources and statistics available on gambling, for example, at **www.begambleaware.org**. They have materials for teachers and youth workers including lesson plans, PowerPoints and other accompanying resources.

Step 4 – Links for further information and extra-curricular opportunities

Extra-curricular opportunities

In addition to the activities identified in the lesson plan builder, there are many opportunities for young people to do work on this topic outside of the curriculum.

Examples include:

- Identify a few companies and following their share price movements over time
- Discuss the different types of insurance cover with their parents/carers and find out what they have insured or decided not to insure
- Research cryptocurrencies to find out how many types there are and what advice they can find for buying them, or not.

Links

- www.londonstockexchange.com
- www.begambleaware.org
- www.moneysavingexpert.com
- www.gamcare.org.uk

ANSWERS:

CASE STUDY: TYPES OF PERSONAL FINANCE RISK PAGE 101

RISK	LOW, MEDIUM OR HIGH RISK?	IMPLICATIONS	HOW TO MINIMISE THE RISK
Giving your debit card to a friend	Medium to high	• They use you card without your knowledge to take money out or make payments with.	• Never give your card or your details to anyone • Always get money out of cash machines yourself.
Putting a friend's PIN into phone notes	High	• They may use without your knowledge • If the same PIN is used for multiple cards or accounts, it could leave you vulnerable to misuse.	• Never give your PIN details to anyone • Never keep records or written notes about your PIN.
Using a holiday company that no one has ever heard of	High	• It may be a scam • The company may not be protected so you would lose your money if the holiday company failed.	• Use an online review site to check the business details • Check if they are ATOL protected • See what other customers think of their service.
Getting a credit card	Low	• Tempting to use and build up debts • Could affect your credit rating if payments are missed.	• Keep the credit limit low • Only use for large purchases • Pay off the balance every month.

ACTIVITY: ASSESSING RISK PAGE 102

How students rank the listed activities will depend on their personal attitudes so there is no right or wrong answer. When considering what risks are associated with each activity, you could discuss:

ACTIVITY	RISK
Crossing a very busy dual carriageway	Being knocked over, causing a driver to be hurt
Sleepover at a friend's house	Food allergies, being tired the next day
Getting a lift in a friend's car	Driving too fast or dangerously
Smoking cigarettes	Health associated risks, fire
Going to watch a Premier League football match	Abusive behaviour, fake tickets
Playing games on a computer	Health and social associated risks
Watching TV	Inappropriate influences, distressing scenes
Riding a bike without a crash helmet	Risk of injury, risk to other who may follow the example
Skydiving	Equipment failure, serious injury or death
Walking down a flight of stairs	Injury risk, spillage

ACTIVITY: ASSESSING RISK OF FINANCIAL DECISIONS **PAGE 103**

Possible answers may include:

- Age 14–18 – choosing a savings account
- Age 17-21 – paying for a holiday with friends and paying rent for accommodation

- Age 20-30 – borrowing money, owning a car, owning a pet
- Late 20s-30s – take out a mortgage
- 30s onwards – plan for retirement

ACTIVITY: INVESTMENTS **PAGE 105**

PERSON	INVESTMENT
1.	Saving would be better than investing, as investments come with risk. Person 1 is not in a position to take risks due to the small amount of disposable income available.
2.	Any investments need to be accessible as they may require the money for their children, so they could consider a medium-term investment plan. Therefore, buying shares may be a possibility.
3.	They should use some of the money to travel and some to invest in shares, property or collective investments. Assuming they have no other debts, they should look at long term investments, possibly property.
4.	She should ensure that she has used up her cash ISA allowance first, to maximise her tax advantages, but as she has savings and no mortgage she could also consider a stocks and shares ISA to invest in a range of shares, bonds and funds. Outside an ISA, she could invest in collective investments to spread the risk or, if she is willing to take more risks, in individual shares or even collectable items like antiques.

CASE STUDY: GAMBLING **PAGE 107**

1. The definition of gambling is playing a game of chance for money with an uncertain outcome. Max is not guaranteed to get the players that he wants if he buys the mystery bundles, so he is taking a chance and is not guaranteed to get the outcome that he wants. Therefore, this is a form of gambling.

2.

- Young people may become addicted to the thrill of not knowing the outcome and this may encourage them to spend more until they get the outcome that they want
- Young people may be tempted to spend more money than they have and may be tempted to use

parents/carers bank cards to pay for games or add-ons etc.

- May encourage young people to consider other forms of gambling.

3. Less likely – he didn't get what he wanted so may not want to take the chance in future.

4. More likely – if he had got all of the players he wanted, he would want to try this again in future.

5. Yes, the mystery bundles are similar to scratch cards, national lottery, betting on horses, cards and casino games. All involve an initial payment but have a random outcome that cannot be predetermined.

CASE STUDY: CRYPTOCURRENCY **PAGE 108**

	PROS	CONS
Option 1 – Buy shares Average 10% rise over past 2 years	• Good return, if past market conditions continue.	• No guarantee that you will make a profit • You could lose a lot of money if the shares perform badly.
Option 2 – Fixed rate savings Guaranteed 2% in 2 years	• Guaranteed return on investment • Better than current 0.5% return.	• Low rate of return (2%) • May be lower than the inflation rate, so the real value of your savings would actually decrease • Cannot withdraw within a 2-year fixed period, without penalties.
Option 3 – Buy cryptocurrency 480% increase in value in 1 year	• Best return on investment if the past market conditions remain and you are prepared to take the risk.	• Extremely high risk. Very volatile market and may fluctuate significantly from day to day • May be difficult to access • Sellers from unregulated sources so no comeback if anything goes wrong.

Based on the pros/cons above, Sandeep and Noor could choose between option 1 (shares) and option 2 (2-year fixed rate savings). Their decision should be determined on the further questions below:

- How much risk are you prepared to take?
- Will you need access to the savings at short notice?
- How long do you want to invest?

Other alternative solutions may include:

- ISAs
- Bonds
- Commodities
- Art, antiques or wine
- Spreading the risk between a number of investments.

ACTIVITY: FINANCIAL PHRASES **PAGE 111**

- **Success and failure are two sides of the same coin** – the likelihood of success and failure is the same.

- **All that glitters is not gold** – just because something looks valuable, doesn't mean it is.

- **Don't throw good money after bad** – don't waste money by spending more money on something that you have already spent money on that is no good (i.e. trying to repair a car that has no value).

- **Money can't buy happiness** – just because you have money, does not mean that you will be happy.

- **Keep the wolf from the door** – just about having enough money to pay for essentials like food and shelter.

- **Don't put all your eggs in one basket** – don't invest in one thing, spread the risk so that you don't lose everything.

- **There's no such thing as a free lunch** – everything has a cost.

- **A debt paid is a friend kept** – paying off debts, keeps everybody happy.

- **Make ends meet** – just about having enough money to get by.

- **Take care of the pennies and the pounds will take care of themselves** – you will always have money if you look after your finances especially the small amounts.

ACTIVITY: SELF-INSURING **PAGE 113**

1. If Andrei self-insures he may not have saved enough money to cover treatment if required and therefore may need some form of borrowing to pay the bill.

2. If Andrei had taken out insurance it would have cost £35 x 12 = £420 for the year. By saving £15 per month, Andrei has saved a total of £15 x 12 = £180. Therefore, making an initial saving already of £240 per year.

   Andrei did not need all of the money he saved because the injections only cost £80, so he has also saved an additional £100 (£180 savings – £80 injections)

3. It would have taken Andrei 6 months to save for the injections.

4. Yes, in this case, Andrei was right to self-insure but only because Casper did not require any other treatment. If Caspar had needed more treatment, or needed the injections before Andrei had saved up £80, then he may have needed to borrow money.

5.
   - Do I have enough money saved to cover an expensive bill?
   - Can I access the money quickly if I need it?
   - What would happen if I lost my job?

DISCUSSION: DOES IT PAY TO BE LOYAL? **PAGE 114**

Chris is more than likely going to get the cheaper insurance because he is a new customer and the insurance company want to encourage him to join them in the first place. Therefore, offering him a great deal in the first year may persuade him to remain with them.

There are no rewards for being loyal whether this is out of a sense of duty or simply due to laziness. Always shop around and get quotes for all your insurance policies. For the majority of people, cheaper quotes can be found, and these quotes can also be used to go back to your current insurer to see if they can match or beat the cheaper prices. Never accept your first renewal quote.

 ## ACTIVITY: INTERESTING INSURANCE **PAGE 114**

Possible answers may include:

- Actors, singers and models insure their important body parts
- Sports stars insure their bodies in the event of injuries
- YouTubers, bloggers and vloggers can insure their equipment, property and voices. They can also be insured if they make statements that are not true!

 ## ACTIVITY: INSURANCE **PAGE 114**

ITEM	POSSIBLE RISKS
House	• Fire/flood damage • Broken into • Broken windows • Paint spilt on carpet.
Car	• Breaks down • Gets stolen • Involved in accident.
Holiday	• Flight cancelled or delayed • Money/camera stolen • Personal injury or accident.

- Mostly the risks are often beyond your control so therefore the likelihood of these things happening really depend on the circumstances. However, the likelihood of a flight being delayed is greater than your house being damaged by a flood.
- All of these risks may be disastrous, upsetting and expensive to the individuals concerned/ involved.
- Yes – for all. Third party motor insurance is legally required if you own and drive a car, but other forms of cover (third party, fire and theft or comprehensive) should be considered. Insurance offers protection against risks, many of which may be beyond your control.
- Pets, phones, health, life, loan/income protection.

CASE STUDY: TYPES OF INSURANCE **PAGE 114**

EMIL	ALIYAH
• Home and contents insurance (for his bike and basic gadgets, but these need to be specified on the policy) • Gadget insurance (yes it exists!) • Phone insurance.	• Specialist travel insurance (covering sports) • Home and contents insurance • Pet insurance • Motor insurance for the campervan.

ANSWERS:
FURTHER YOUR KNOWLEDGE

SELLING SHARES PAGE 118

INVESTOR	TYPE OF TAX	AMOUNT OF TAX
1. Danah	Stamp Duty Reserve Tax Capital Gains Tax	£11,800 x 0.5% = £59 Profit is £23,650 - £11,800 = £11,850 Profit-allowance= £11,850-£11,700 = £150 Danah will pay 10% capital gains tax on £150. Her tax will be £15
2. Emily	Stamp Duty Reserve Tax	£4,250 x 0.5% = £21.25 Rounded up = £25
3. Juan	Capital Gains Tax	He will pay no tax as his gain is below the threshold
4. Oliver	Stamp Duty Reserve Tax	£6,100 x 0.5% = £30.50

INSURANCE PAGE 119

1. If Joel had decided to purchase the insurance, how much would the phone and insurance have cost him for the 2-year contract?

Phone cost = £60 x 24 months = £1,440

Insurance = £100 per year x 2 = £200

TOTAL = £1,640

2. Joel decides to replace his phone with the same model and learning from this mistake, he decides he will also take out mobile phone insurance to prevent any future possible damages or theft. How much has this whole experience cost him?

Payment of original contract + purchase of new phone + insurance = **£2,640**

3. Yes, in this case it would have saved Joel £1,000 and the trouble of having to sort out his broken phone. However, if he had been more careful he would not have needed to replace his phone, but clearly this was the risk that he decided to take.

If he had never damaged his phone, over the lifetime of the contract, he could have saved £200, but due to the fact that the phone is so expensive this is something he should have considered more. Perhaps if he had purchased a cheaper phone he may not have needed to consider the insurance.

4. Why do you think this figure is so low?
- It is not compulsory
- People are prepared to take the risk
- Some people would rather use any savings that they might have to replace/repair their phone if it is damaged or stolen.

INVESTING IN SHARES PAGE 120

1.

COMPANY NAME	NO. OF SHARES OWNED BY SANDEEP AND NOOR	PRICE BOUGHT PER SHARE (IN P)	VALUE OF INVESTMENT (£)	PRICE TODAY (IN P)	TODAY'S VALUE OF INVESTMENT (£)
The Blue Company	2500	6p	£150	7p	£175
YellowSquare	48	725p	£348	722p	£346.56
Green Edit PLC	150	140p	£210	139p	£208.50
Red-Champ	500	58p	£290	56p	£280
TOTAL			£998		£1,010.06

2. The Blue Company are the only profitable shares. Sandeep and Noor made £25 profit. They bought the shares for £150 and today they are valued at £175.

3. How much profit or loss have Sandeep and Noor made in total from when they purchased the shares?

They bought all of their shares for £998 and today they are worth £1,010.06. Therefore, they have made a profit of £12.06.

4. Today's price for YellowSquare shares is 722p. If the price falls by 10%, the new price would be 649.8p (722p-72.2p). Rounded to 650p.

Today's price for Green Edit PLC shares is 139p. If the price increases by 15%, the new price would be 159.85p (139p+20.85p). Rounded to 160p.

The value of their portfolio is now:

COMPANY NAME	NO. OF SHARES OWNED BY SANDEEP AND NOOR	NEW PRICE (IN P)	NEW VALUE OF INVESTMENT (£)
The Blue Company	2500	7p	£175
YellowSquare	48	650p	£312
Green Edit PLC	150	160p	£240
Red-Champ	500	56p	£280
TOTAL			£1,007

The changes in prices has resulted in a decrease in the value of their portfolio by **£3.06**

5.
- Not guaranteed to make a profit so may lose money
- May decide to sell at the wrong time
- Need to invest in the long term to see real gains, which may mean keeping your money in the investment for longer than you want to
- External, unexpected factors can affect the price of shares meaning that the value is beyond your control.

SECURITY AND FRAUD

What does this chapter cover?

This chapter considers what is meant by identity theft and fraud, how fraud can be carried out and what young people can do to protect themselves from it.

The following topics are explored either through the provision of information and case studies, or through activities for students. Alongside each topic is a possible curriculum link:

TOPIC	CURRICULUM LINK					
	PSHEE				CITIZENSHIP	MATHEMATICS
	MANAGING RISK	BEING A CRITICAL CONSUMER	WIDER IMPACT OF PURCHASING CHOICES	CONSUMER RIGHTS AND REDRESS		
What we mean by identity theft and the history of it	■				■	■
What is fraud	■				■	
The different methods used to carry out identity theft					■	
The terminology used in carrying out fraud					■	
Tactics to stop a fraud occurring	■				■	
Fake emails and how to spot them	■					
Fake websites	■					
How to protect yourself against online shopping fraud		■				
What happens if someone does steal your identity			■	■		
How to protect yourself against identity theft	■					
Passwords and security questions	■					■
Biometric verification	■					
Sources of help for victims of identity theft				■	■	

WHY IS THIS TOPIC IMPORTANT FOR YOUNG PEOPLE?

In 2017, identity fraud victims aged **21** or under increased by **30%**

Source: www.cifas.org.uk

In 2017, **83%** of identity frauds were perpetrated online, which places tech savvy **young people at greater risk.**

Source: www.cifas.org.uk

29% of the **18-24 age group** are willing to share their mother's maiden name (a common security question) online with their friends.

Source: www.rbs.com

The number of **18-24 year-olds** being tricked into using their bank account to transfer the proceeds of crime has increased by **75%**

Source: www.cifas.org.uk

LESSON PLAN BUILDER

Step 1 – Pick a starter activity
(10 – 15 minutes)

Fraud terminology PSHE CITIZENSHIP

A simple starter activity is to identify some words and phrases used to describe a fraud. Some examples include: cheat, con, confidence trick, dodge, fiddle, fix, hoax, racket, rip off, rob, scam, sham, sting, and swindle. These could be put into a word search using one of the many word search generators that are available online, or you could choose some or all of these and make anagrams of them for students to find the correct word or phrase.

Initially you could set a target, of say six, and help the class with the rest to ensure the starter activity does not take too long to complete.

How fraudsters get personal information from your computer CITIZENSHIP

The exercise on how well they understand computer terminology is a great starter exercise for the class (see page 125). After the definitions have been matched to the terms, follow up by asking students how these can get onto their computer.

Bad passwords PSHE CITIZENSHIP MATHEMATICS

The activity on the top 10 worst passwords (see page 132) makes a good starter. You could ask for a show of hands from the whole class to see what they think are the worst five before giving them the actual order.

There is an opportunity to look at the probability of guessing a 4-digit PIN and extending this by considering the most common PINs (an internet search will reveal many articles on this) and how people using common PINs makes life much easier for a fraudster.

Protecting yourself from identity theft and fraud PSHE CITIZENSHIP

The list of 10 ways to protect yourself from fraud (see page 131) can be used as a starter activity to find out which ones students are aware of and which ones they do themselves.

Find out if there are any other tips that they know of that they can share with the rest of the class.

YouTube videos PSHE CITIZENSHIP MATHEMATICS

The information on what to do if your identity is stolen (see page 130) and the subsequent activity and discussions on support available (see page 134) gives the opportunity for students to explore the Action Fraud website, and the range of freely-available short videos on YouTube.

You should explore these at an early stage in teaching identity theft and fraud as there are a number that would make excellent starters to a number of the topics covered in the textbook. For example, the "Data to go" video produced by Cifas would make an excellent starter activity to any work on social media fraud.

Step 2 – Pick a core activity/activities
(25 – 30 minutes)

What is meant by identity theft and fraud PSHE CITIZENSHIP MATHEMATICS

The topic of security and fraud is an ever-changing area resulting in new terminology being created all the time, so a good starting point for this topic is to make it clear what is meant by identity theft and fraud. The information sections on these could be read to the class by you or read in pairs/groups with you following up with questions like the three provided in the textbook (see page 122).

Using the links for further information, gather data on trends in identity theft over the years and use this for work on number and solving problems in a financial context.

Email scams PSHE

The three examples of email scams should be read by students either individually or with one group member reading to others in the group (see page 126). In a follow-up discussion, students could be asked which ones they think are scams (they all are) and to rank them in order of which one they feel people are most likely to believe.

They could also consider which people are most likely to do as the email asks, for example, would it be a certain age? Or gender? Or people with particular personal characteristics?

Fraud case studies PSHE CITIZENSHIP

The three case studies all have questions that can be used in class or group discussion (see pages 128, 130, 135). Instead of discussing the answer to the questions, you could ask students/pairs/groups to identify three things that could have been done in each situation. You can then collate these ideas and produce agreed strategies with the class.

What happens when your identity is stolen PSHE

The information on what happens if someone steals your identity will need to be explained to students, especially the various terms like credit history and credit score (definitions of these terms can be found in the Borrowing chapter), which may well be new to students (see page 61). Using a case study of a young person who fell victim to identity theft would be one way to explain these terms. Students could be asked to represent the various credit terms through a spidergram containing pictures and symbols.

This activity could be linked to the information on "10 top tips to protect yourself against identity theft" and follow-up questions (see page 131). These questions could be done individually, or in pairs, so that students can compare answers with their friends and classmates.

Choosing a password PSHE MATHEMATICS

Students will already have a number of passwords themselves, so before discussing the password top tips (see page 132) it would be a worthwhile exercise to ask students to come up with their own tips on writing and using passwords. Then compare what they have said with the textbook. Following the advice on characteristics of a good security question (see page 132), students could be asked to devise their own.

Step 3 – Pick an extension activity
(10 – 15 minutes)

Ghost broking

A growing area of fraud is that of ghost broking, where fraudsters pretend to offer very cheap car insurance but instead leave large numbers of individuals and organisations without insurance. Students could be asked to research this to find out:

- How the fraud is carried out
- What the consequences can be for victims
- How to avoid ghost broking

The City of London Police website **www.cityoflondonpolice.uk** is an excellent source of information about this type of fraud.

Social media fraud

Social media is an area that fraudsters target to get personal information. Unfortunately, many people are still very naive with the information they put onto social media. Students could use the internet to research things that people do on social media and report what they find back to the class. A short TV ad produced by Barclays on digital safety can be found online and demonstrates the personal information a fraudster can extract from social media.

Phone scams

Phone scams and text message scams are often aimed at young people – students could research the "Take Five to Stop Fraud" website to find advice on how to avoid these types of frauds. They also have an online test that students could take to see if they might be taken in by a scam.

Step 4 – Links for further information and extra-curricular opportunities

Extra-curricular opportunities

In addition to the activities identified in the lesson plan builder, there are many opportunities for young people to do work on this topic outside of the curriculum.

Examples include:
- Reviewing their own privacy settings on social media
- Using the Facebook security check up
- Changing their passwords, in particular those which they use more than once or those which they feel a fraudster could work out

- Talking to other family members about their own experiences of identity fraud
- Using their own improved awareness of tactics to prevent fraud with other family members who may be less confident with IT than they are.

Links

- www.cifas.org.uk
- www.takefive-stopfraud.org.uk
- www.actionfraud.police.uk
- www.financialfraudaction.org.uk
- www.moneymules.co.uk

ANSWERS:

ACTIVITY: TYPES OF IDENTITY THEFT PAGE 124

METHOD OF FRAUD	TACTICS TO STOP THE FRAUD
Bank card skimming	Don't let anyone take your card away to make a purchase. Always cover your hand when putting your PIN into an ATM to withdraw cash.
Bank card scanning	Keep cards all together in a wallet or bag (scanners cannot read multiple cards). Keep cards in front pockets (not back). Thieves prefer to scan your card from behind as you are unlikely to see them doing it.
Theft	Keep bags zipped up. Use bags that go over the shoulder. Don't put wallets in your back pocket.
Bin raiding/ changing address	Shred all documents which contain your personal details. Receive all statements and bills online.
Hacking	Keep accounts secure by using passwords that are difficult to guess. Change your passwords often.
Malware	Install a firewall. Install antivirus software.
Phishing	Never click on unknown links or pop-ups. Avoid responding to emails that do not seem legitimate.
Vishing	Never give anyone personal details over the phone. Check phone numbers online to check if they are legitimate.
Smishing	Do not click on any links or reply to numbers that you do not recognise. Never forward personal details in an email or text.

ACTIVITY: TERMINOLOGY PAGE 125

1 = Virus **2** = Trojan **3** = Bots **4** = Worm **5** = Spyware **6** = Adware **7** = Ransomware

ACTIVITY: SPOTTING FAKE EMAILS **PAGE 126**

METHOD OF FRAUD	TACTICS TO STOP THE FRAUD
Email 1	• If it sounds too good to be true – it usually is • Any request for bank details should be seen as suspicious • Unofficial email address provided • No other details about Alejandro and Pedro given.
Email 2	• Poor spelling and grammar • Generic email address • Not addressed to you by name, only "Dear friend" • No details of the person/business given.
Email 3	• Not addressed to you by name, only "Dear user" • Poor grammar and lack of punctuation • If it was legitimate, their email address would not be **mail.check@netscape.com**.

 CASE STUDY: CYBERCRIME **PAGE 128**

Jess and her mum could have avoided this fraud by:

1. Only paying for items where you see a secure payment service – look for a URL starting with "https" and a closed padlock symbol.

2. Only using verified payment providers such as PayPal, which helps to protect you. Never do a bank transfer with people you don't know.

3. Check the website address to make sure it is genuine.

4. When using retail websites, find out exactly who you are dealing with.

5. Visit the homepage of the website or the "About us" pages and read the text there. Watch out for poor English, such as spelling and grammar mistakes, or phrases that don't sound quite right.

6. Make sure you read the feedback on the website about the seller.

7. Check the item's description carefully – ask the seller questions if you're not sure of something.

8. Be extremely careful when buying things from people with little or no selling history.

ACTIVITY: PROTECTING YOURSELF AGAINST ONLINE SHOPPING FRAUD
PAGE 129

1. Padlock, PayPal **2.** Slightly **3.** UK **4.** English, Phone number **5.** Feedback **6.** Description **7.** History

CASE STUDY: WHAT HAPPENS IF SOMEONE STEALS YOUR IDENTITY PAGE 130

- Receive all statements and bills online
- Check statements regularly and use secure apps to track spending
- Check your credit report

- If possible, move the letterboxes to a more secure area inside the building
- Pick up mail regularly or, if they go on holiday, ask a friend or a neighbour they know well to collect it.

ACTIVITY: PASSWORDS PAGE 132

Passwords – the five worst passwords in order are:

1) 123456
2) password
3) 12345
4) 12345678
5) football

Suggested rules:

- Do not use the same password for more than one account
- Never write down your passwords or put notes on your phone
- Never use passwords that are easy to guess

DISCUSSION: OTHER TYPES OF FRAUD PAGE 134

Charity donation fraud: Could affect you if you donate to a cause in person or online that isn't real.

Mobile phone fraud: Could affect you if you receive a text message or email that looks like it is from a reputable brand asking you to provide your bank details or make a payment, and you do so.

Romance fraud: Online dating and social media can provide the opportunity for people to not be truthful about their true identity. Care should be taken around discussions with anyone not directly known to you, and any discussion about sending money should be treated as highly suspicious.

CASE STUDY: FAKE WEBSITES **PAGE 135**

- Only buy tickets from the venue's box office, the promoter, an official agent or a well-known and reputable ticket exchange site

- Should you choose to buy tickets from an individual (for example via an online auction site or social media), you should pay using a secure payment service. Avoid making payments through bank transfer or money transfer services, as the payment may not be recoverable

- Paying for your tickets by credit card will offer increased protection over other payments methods, such as debit card, cash, or money transfer services

- Check the contact details of the site you're buying the tickets from. There should be a landline phone number and a full postal address

- Check the web address to make sure you're on the correct website. Any webpages you enter personal or financial details into should start with "https" and display a locked padlock icon in the address bar.

ACTIVITY: MONEY MULES **PAGE 136**

1. The job advert is unlikely to be genuine for a number of reasons:

- No business name/logo
- No job title
- No address or name given
- No landline given, only a mobile phone number to text
- No application process (e.g. CV, letter) – how will they find out about you and your previous experience, qualifications etc?
- If it seems too good to be true, it usually is.

2. There are a number of people you could report it to:

- Report it to the "Action Fraud" helpline
- Report it to the police.

3. The factsheet could contain:

- Be wary of people who contact you through social media who don't know you
- Never give your bank account details to anyone who you do not trust or know
- Be wary of offers of money, particularly if there is no job title, business or job information
- Be wary of job offers that you haven't applied for
- If you do receive a job offer, always check to make sure the business is genuine
- Research any job offers you get, particularly if the business only operates online or overseas
- Avoid any job advert if the use of English is poor.

ANSWERS:
FURTHER YOUR KNOWLEDGE

PERSONAL DATA PAGE 138

1. 40% + 32% = 72%

2. a) 16-24 (88%), 25-34 (80%), 35-44 (77%)

b)
- Younger people tend to be more confident in using technology
- They are more likely to understand the importance of protecting oneself online
- Younger age groups are more likely to have received some education in protecting oneself online.

3. a) 65-74 (18%)

b) Yes because:

- 65-74 year-olds are more likely to be less confident at managing their data online
- This age group are less likely to understand the importance of protecting their personal details online/perhaps more vulnerable
- Less likely to understand the implications of protecting their details online
- Less likely to have received any training or education about protecting oneself online.

4.

	TOTAL	VERY CONFIDENT	FAIRLY CONFIDENT	NEITHER/DON'T KNOW	NOT VERY CONFIDENT	NOT AT ALL CONFIDENT
Males	900	392 – 44%	288 – 32%	80 – 9%	80 – 9%	60 – 6%
Females	900	333 – 37%	288 – 32%	99 – 11%	99 – 11%	81 – 9%

5. Males are more likely to feel confident (76%) at managing their personal data online compared to 69% of females. 20% of females asked felt that they were not confident at managing their personal data online compared to 16% of males.

CHECKS MADE PAGE 139

1. Internet users are also asked about the types of checks they make when buying online, before entering their debit or credit card details. Two in three internet users who say they buy things online (67%) say they check to see if the site looks secure, while more than half check whether they are familiar with the company or brand (56%) or check whether there is a link to another reputable service (53%).

One in three check to see if there is a guarantee that their details will not be shared with anyone (33%) and one in four rely on recommendations from their friends or family (24%). Three quarters of internet users don't make any of these checks (74%)

15% of those who purchase online say they look to see if the site they are purchasing from is listed on a search engine and one in 10 (11%) say that they go ahead anyway if it is the only way to get what they want. 5% say they enter their credit or debit card details online whenever they are asked for; this is more likely for 25-34 year-olds. One quarter of internet users (24%) who purchase online say they do at least one of these three things.

TEST YOUR GDPR KNOWLEDGE PAGE 140

1. Answer b)
The above plus medical records, social network data and bank details

2. Answer a)
They must tell you how you can order them to delete all of the personal data that they hold about you

3. Answer c)
Anything that will help save your life

4. Answer c)
Inform the authorities within 72 hours of it happening

5. Answer c)
They can only use it in the way that was explained to you before you gave them consent to use it

FURTHER HELP
AND SUPPORT

The following pages provide details of some of the organisations that can provide further help and support in developing and delivering high quality financial education within your school.

THE LONDON INSTITUTE OF BANKING & FINANCE

The London Institute of Banking & Finance

About Us

We exist for a very simple reason – to advance banking and finance by providing outstanding education and thinking. Our focus is on lifelong learning, starting in schools with life skills and reaching across an industry professional's career.

And because we've been at the heart of the sector since 1879, we create connections and build partnerships that make banking and finance more accessible and understood.

What we do

Our financial capability qualifications equip students with the knowledge and confidence they need to make good financial decisions, as well as inspiring the next generation of finance and banking professionals.

We provide students with rigorous qualifications which develop resilient young people who are able to progress into higher education, further education or employment. Students not only learn how to manage their money effectively, they also learn about income and expenditure, credit and debt, insurance, savings and pensions, financial products, and how public money is raised and spent; helping them prepare for financial independence.

Every school gets a dedicated Customer Relationship Manager to help you map out your delivery and support you every step of the way. Our programmes are specifically designed with the busy teacher in mind – helping you fit this vital subject into your timetable.

We are also working with vulnerable people and charities across the UK to give everybody access to essential financial skills.

How to get in touch

To find out more or to arrange a visit to your school, email **fccrm@libf.ac.uk** or call us on **01227 828234**.

THE MONEY CHARITY

About Us

The Money Charity is the UK's financial capability charity. Our vision is that everyone has the ability to be on top of their money as a part of everyday life. We empower adults and young people across the UK to build the skills, knowledge, attitudes and behaviours to make the most of their money throughout their lives.

What we do

We can help teachers deliver financial education in three main ways:

Money Workshops

Our interactive Money Workshops are delivered in schools and colleges to KS3, KS4 and Post 16 students by financial education experts. The workshops equip students with the skills they need to make the right financial decisions for them, now and in the future. They are mapped to the curriculum and cover budgeting, debt, saving, insurance, pensions, pay slips, mortgages and much more!

The Student MoneyManual

Our Student MoneyManual helps give students all the key information they need to manage their money at uni, including details on the student finance package, repaying loans and living on a student budget. It is aimed at those who are already studying at uni and also Year 12/13 students who are considering it.

Teacher Resource Packs

Our Teacher Resource Packs are designed to equip teachers with activities and resources so they can deliver financial education lessons themselves, with as little prep as possible required. Each pack contains 1 hour of content divided into 3 activities, mapped to the national curriculum. There are packs specifically designed for KS3 and KS4, covering budgeting, planning, saving, credit, getting paid, banking, and more!

How to get in touch

Much of what we do is free to schools! Get in touch to find out what we can do to help your school deliver effective financial education.

youngpeople@themoneycharity.org.uk
0207 062 8933
www.themoneycharity.org.uk

THE NATIONAL SKILLS ACADEMY FOR FINANCIAL SERVICES

The National **Skills** Academy

FINANCIAL SERVICES

About Us

We are an employer-led charity that works with the financial services industry to; support skills development in the sector, help people from disadvantaged communities access jobs in the industry and improve the financial capability of the wider UK population.

What we do

We have a range of training programmes that are designed to equip people with the skills needed to support others to develop their money management skills.

Our courses include Life, Money, Action!, a level 2 accredited qualification for people wanting to develop the skills needed to support young people aged 16-24 with their money management, particularly as they approach key life transitions, such as starting work, an apprenticeship or further/higher education.

We also have a range of digital resources that help young people develop their skills and knowledge on a range of money related topics. These can be used by young people independently or with the support of school staff and are available free of charge at lifemoneyaction.nsafs.co.uk

We can also work with your school to develop financial capability training to meet its specific needs.

How to get in touch

You can find out more about the National Skills Academy by visiting **nsafs.co.uk**.

If you have any enquires please contact us at: **info@nsafs.co.uk** or by calling **0845 618 2353**.

MYBNK

About Us

MyBnk is a UK charity which provides a range of financial education programmes for 7-25 year olds in schools and youth organisations. Ideal for PSHE, Citizenship, Maths and Business students.

What we do

Together with young people, MyBnk has created innovative, high impact and high energy workshops that bring money to life.

MyBnk's experts can come to your school armed with the latest resources and techniques to help students learn how to manage money, navigate the financial system and understand tax, debt, career choices and student finance.

All sessions use real life case studies, colourful resources, games, videos and links to popular culture.

They are delivered by fully trained, tested and DBS cleared staff, are closely mapped to the national curriculum and are proven and evaluated by the government's Money Advice Service.

Workshops are available as double lessons or half day sessions and can be delivered to an entire year group or a single class.

Programmes:

Money Twist - KS3-5

Format: 3x100 minute workshops. Can be delivered on off-timetable days. Group size: 12-30.

Segmented for 11-14 and 14-18 year olds in secondary schools, Money Twist covers a range of practical and relevant everyday financial matters including budgeting, needs vs wants, careers, tax, banking, interest, savings, pensions and investments.

MyBnk also offers a sporty version of this programme. Ideal for an outside play area or a sports hall.

Uni Dosh

Format: 2 hour workshop. Group size: 12-30.

Aimed at 16-18 year olds considering going to university, Uni Dosh offers a comprehensive overview of student finance, banking, employment, tax, and the importance of budgeting when living independently.

How to get in touch

Contact **info@mybnk.org**
or visit **www.mybnk.org/our-work**